Goat Water
Is Not What You Think

The Montserrat Island Life
of Two Hoosiers
and the Volcano That Ended It

Carol Elrod

Hawthorne Publishing
Carmel, Indiana

ISBN 978-0-9912095-0-7

Hawthorne Publishing
15601 Oak Road
Indianapolis
IN 46033
317-867-5183
www.hawthornepub.com

Printed and bound in the United States of America

Dedication

For Ed, my husband and best friend,

and for Scott, Diana, Molly and Emily

ACKNOWLEDGMENTS

This book has been percolating in my mind for a long time. I kept diaries of our winters on Montserrat, but didn't quite know what I was going to do with them. I was encouraged by my husband Ed and by friends in the States to find a way to share our story.

I knew that what happened to Ed and me during those four years was very different from what most people experience. Who, for example, has sung in a choir concert with bats zipping back and forth overhead? And who has witnessed the build-up to volcanic eruptions less than three miles up a mountain from home? During our time on Montserrat, we learned to live with less, to accept what we did not or could not have, to take joy in simple pleasures, to live close to the land and to be in sync with nature.

We have our Montserratian and our Canadian friends to thank for the example they set. We will always be grateful to them.

All the events in this book really happened, but the names have been changed to protect the innocent and, sometimes, the guilty.

INTRODUCTION

Montserrat, shaped like a teardrop, is about ten miles long and seven miles wide at its widest point. Like many islands in the Caribbean, it is volcanic, meaning it was formed millions of years ago by eruptions under the sea, which eventually pushed lava upwards until land was exposed. When my husband Ed and I became acquainted with Montserrat, ordinary people on the island thought the mountains were quiet.

The fact that Montserrat had hot springs—and tourists came for spa treatments—didn't bother anybody. In some areas of the island, sulfur was being extruded from the earth, but the general population thought this to be a boon for tourism and a curiosity, nothing more. Some scientists took another view, but their conclusions were buried in the literature—or unheeded. The tallest mountain was Chance's Peak at 3,002 feet above sea level. It was near the sulfur beds, which were on the Westside of Montserrat south of the capital city, Plymouth.

The islands of the Caribbean, including St. Thomas, Antigua, Guadeloupe, Dominica, Martinique, Barbados and Trinidad, to name some that are well-known to tourists, form a curved chain leading from Puerto Rico south toward South America. Montserrat is much less well known than the larger islands and is not even noted on some maps.

Because of Montserrat's laid-back lifestyle and the lack of air traffic overhead, George Martin, the Beatles arranger and record producer, built a large recording studio on the island, and the Fab Four and other performers came there to rehearse and record. We were told that the Montserratians didn't pay much attention to the celebrities in their midst and let them relax and work in peace. This studio was destroyed by Hurricane Hugo on September 17, 1989, and the George Martin era came to an end.

Way back in its history, from perhaps 500 BC until 500 AD, Montserrat was the home of Arawak Indians, who came from South America by canoe and established an advanced civilization. In the 1400s, the principal indigenous Indians were the more war-like Caribs. Many of the remaining Indians on the island died of diseases brought by Spanish explorers. Christopher Columbus, who first saw the island during his second voyage to the New World in 1493, named the tear-shaped Caribbean jewel "Montserrat." The reason?

The serrated mountains reminded him of those in the vicinity of the Santa Maria de Montserrate monastery near Barcelona, Spain.

White Irish/Catholic settlers, escapees from persecution on the nearby island of St. Kitts, arrived on Montserrat in the 1600s. They either brought along or procured slaves for their sugar and cotton plantations. Descendants of those slaves are the Montserratians of today. Many of the slaves took the last names of their owners, and descendants even now have Irish surnames, such as Riley, Ryan and O'Garro. And Montserrat is called the "Other Emerald Isle," partly because of its Irish past and partially because the mountains are so green.

Over time, ownership of the island shifted back and forth between the French and the British. It was returned to the British as part of the Treaty of Versailles in 1783. Although other islands in the Caribbean later became independent, Montserrat voted to remain a dependency of Great Britain in 1962.

Ed and I came upon this island paradise after the hurricane. A Category 4 storm, Hurricane Hugo killed 10 people on Montserrat and caused $250 million in damage. Guadeloupe was also severely affected, and as the storm moved northwest, so were the US Virgin Islands, Puerto Rico and South Carolina. Charleston was especially hard-hit.

As many as 11,000 Montserratians were left homeless. In fact, almost all the island's buildings were damaged to some degree. A couple of weeks after the hurricane, a Methodist minister friend asked Ed to join him and others from central and southern Indiana to help rebuild houses. During his week-long stay, Ed grew to love the smashed-up island.

He took me back for a vacation the next year and the year after that, after which we bought a small house on the Eastside of the island. I had not seen it at the time we purchased it. Ed saw the house the first time when he went to sign the papers. We chose that area because that's where he had worked and that's where he already knew people. Nearly all of the people he knew were residents of Montserratian villages up the flanks of Chance's Peak, and of "Spanish Point," a subdivision down the mountain toward the Atlantic Ocean. (The Westside of the island faces the Caribbean Sea.) Those living in Spanish Point, where our house-to-be was located, were not necessarily all people native to the Island. There were also what people on the island called expatriates.

Expatriates, or "expats" on this island, meant people who weren't native to the island but chose to live there full—or part-time. Most expats were white. Not many of them lived on the Eastside of the island, but some, like us, did.

The social life of white enclaves on the Westside of the island tended to center on the Montserrat Golf Club. Some of the houses, but by no means all, were large and luxurious. There was a lot of partying among the expats in the West, not so much in the East.

Westsiders preferred to stay near the golf club and the capital city, Plymouth, where most of the shops were. Because the roads on the island were curvy, there were drop-offs, animals ran loose and streetlights were almost non-existent, many expats didn't like to drive at night. This was one major reason why the expats from the two sides of the island didn't know each other very well.

Westside subdivisions and towns were not segregated, however. Montserratians with more money tended to live near expats who had more money. Stratification definitely was by class, not by race. Lower middle class and poor Montserratians lived in both the West and the East.

Ed and I purchased our house after seeing a video prepared by a neighbor who was acting as an agent for the seller, a Canadian widower in his 80s who had decided he needed to return to his home country to be near relatives. After our initial visits to the island and our decision to look for a home, Ed had done a walk-through of the home we selected before he signed the papers in February of 1992. I was eager to see it. A life completely foreign to anything we had known growing up in Indianapolis, Indiana, was about to begin.

Now for some geography …

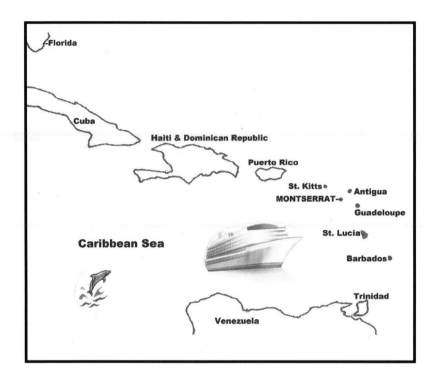

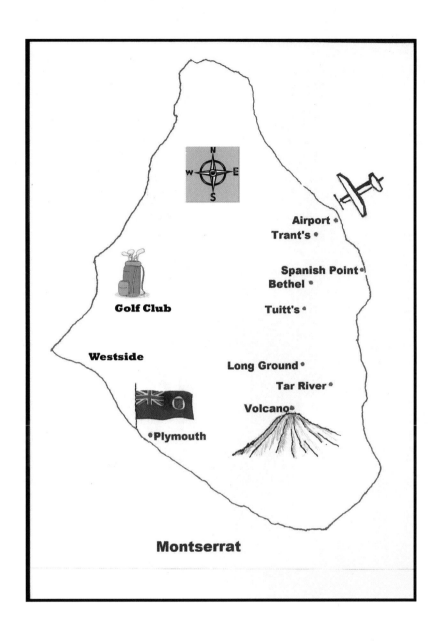

Montserrat

1
RETIREMENT PLAN

Prepared for our month-long visit to the island, with small suitcases containing not much more than swimsuits and shorts, we opened the door of our new home one evening shortly after dark. When we turned on a light, cockroaches the size of mice skittered up the living room walls. It was April 1, 1992.

I had taken a month's vacation from my job as a newspaper reporter on *The Indianapolis Star*, and we flew to Montserrat, leaving our dog in a kennel and our cat in the care of a neighbor near our home in Indianapolis. Having purchased this island house, our intent was to try out the island lifestyle before we actually retired and flew down to spend half a year. Ed, a life insurance agent, could conduct business anywhere in the world via phone and fax. At that time, we weren't connected to the Internet.

This was our initiation to life in the tropics. On that first night, cockroaches seemed to be a disgusting, but minor, glitch, although the can of bug repellant we found under the kitchen sink was nearly empty. We spent the better part of our first hour attempting to kill what roaches we could by stepping on them. Not only could they outrun us, but stepping on them seemed to do no good. They were just stunned and retreated behind the baseboards, into the drawers and behind the pictures on the walls where they'd been spending their time. It is said cockroaches have survived since the time of the dinosaurs, and we learned why that night. Our attempts at mass murder were going to take a while.

Before unpacking anything, I sat down with a pad of paper and pencil to start a shopping list for our first trip into Plymouth, which was on the other side of the island from us. It was a trip we would often make, twelve miles round-trip. Raid was first on the list. Then we walked from room to room to see what our "villa" contained; it had been sold to us "furnished." And also, it was turning out, the place was sold "as is."

We soon found out that the previous owner saved everything, no matter what condition it was in. He was old and tired, and he did not repair much of anything, so there were enough nonfunctional items in the house to keep a handyman busy for years. The TV set didn't work, and the small boom box radio worked, but the tape deck in it didn't. Lamp cords had been cut and spliced back together in the middle, some window cranks were missing, and the springs in the couch had long since given up. None of these things showed on the video we had seen back in the Hoosier State.

The man's wife had died a few years before, and the house certainly suffered from the lack of what one of the neighbors called "a woman's touch." On the other hand, one kitchen cabinet held a complete set of Royal Doulton china. I was a little disappointed in our house purchase by this time, but finding the Royal Doulton made me feel somewhat better. Maybe buying the place wasn't such a huge mistake. I believed that even more when Ed suggested we go for a swim and never mind the unpacking, which could wait until the next day.

He took off his clothes in the middle of the living room—and didn't put anything back on. He convinced me no one would see, since it was dark, and that it would be okay. To get to the pool, we had only to walk out the front door and down two steps, he said.

All my negative thoughts were washed away as I sloshed around in the bathtub temperature water and looked up and saw the sky full of stars.

The little house had no air conditioning, but it didn't matter because of the breeze coming off the ocean 800 yards or so away and down the hill. We made up the bed after our swim and crawled in.

The next morning, after breakfast of coffee, bread, butter and eggs left for us by the real estate agent/neighbor and his wife, we toured the yard to see what plants came with the place. We didn't know what many of them were. We could pick out hibiscus, of course, and the whole yard was ringed with hibiscus bushes, all in bloom, and of many varieties. We also had five coconut palms full-grown and three that had sprouted only recently. But there were many mysteries, too, in the garden of the house we would come to call "Paradise East."

We soon learned that Will Tolbert, the former owner of our house, apparently had a habit of throwing coconuts just over the fence, and many of these had sprouted. On our first pass through the yard, I gathered up an armful of plastic margarine and whipped topping containers and threw them in the trash.

Before we flew down to take possession of the house, we learned that it had been broken into. We were assured that it was petty thievery and that only a sheet, a pair of scissors, and a bottle of salad oil were taken. The neighbor who sold us the house, Vic Henry, said the thief probably wouldn't be back, as there wasn't anything of value taken or desired. I guessed that Royal Doulton wouldn't be high on any thief's list.

The shopping list for town grew ever longer as we rid drawers of dead roaches and dusted closet shelves so we could put our clothes away. I threw away the bedside table in our bedroom. It had only three legs and was propped against the wall so it wouldn't fall over.

This is only a partial list of what we decided we needed on that first shopping foray: Lamp cord with which to replace all the "country cousin" wiring, a deadbolt for our back door, a shovel, a doormat, a garbage can, brooms to replace those that were worn to a nub, and a padlock and chain for our front gate.

Later, neighbors told us that thievery such as had happened to us had been going on for years, and white and black alike were victims. Thieves apparently had no intention of confronting a homeowner, and most did their deeds under cover of darkness when no one was home. On some occasions, however, homeowners playing cards in the living room were unaware that, at the same time, someone had slit the screen (or reached through louvers) in the bedroom and stolen any wallet or purse that could be reached.

In our case, the thief or thieves removed a couple of the wooden louvers from our back door, bent the screen and reached in to unlock the door. We hoped that deadbolts would provide a deterrent. Realistically, we knew the locks would only help, not solve the problem. After all, we had glass louvers in some windows, and these could easily be removed, too. In addition, the house was isolated. High bushes in the vacant pasture behind our house screened us from the neighbor to the west, and the house next door on the other side was owned by a couple who lived in England.

While cleaning out, we learned more and more about what

household goods we had inherited. There was a large stack of ironed linen tablecloths, napkins, and guest towels, many of them embroidered. Most were stained, however, and some had holes in them. All smelled of mildew. I threw away broken glass candlesticks and an ash tray that had been shattered and painstakingly glued back together, although there were pieces missing.

Along the way, we learned from neighbors that many of the house's furnishings, to include the dishes, the cut glass, the silver and the crystal had belonged to the original owners of the house, the Caubles. One of most interest to me was an oil portrait of a woman, perhaps in the style of the late 1700s. She was knitting booties and was dressed in black with a bonnet on her head. The painter, according to the signature, was Amy Howard Porteous or Pontius or Pontious. I never could find out anything about her or about the painting, which was created in either 1808 or 1810. The date was hard to read.

Originally, there were two paintings, of this woman and another of a man, but when that original owner Cauble, who was then a widower of about 80, died of a combination of alcohol and pills, a relative took the painting of the man off island. The scuttlebutt in Spanish Point was that the paintings were of Cauble's ancestors.

The painting was not in very good shape. The canvas was cracked, and there were two holes in it, possibly received when the painting blew off the wall during Hurricane Hugo. Rolling it up to transport it to the United States for repairs would have been dangerous, I decided. There were no art conservators on island. And so the painting of the unknown woman would stay on the wall, probably disintegrating more and more as the years went by due to the heat, the humidity, and whatever else Nature had in mind.

Although the TV was broken when we arrived on island, we found a policeman who repaired electronics in his spare time. Without a daily newspaper, an informational mainstay for us back in the States, we had no idea what was going on in the world without television or radio. At that, we didn't have cable TV on Montserrat, so we were stuck with one station—ABS from Antigua, across the "pond" 27 miles away. It broadcast world news—with snippets from the States—at 6:30 a.m., and we always tried to watch. But we could go for days and not see or hear any US news.

Early in our one-month stay, we spent a lot of time trying to get rid of a large "wood slave," a transparent, grayish-pink lizard which had been hiding out behind pictures on our walls, particularly behind the large painting of the old woman. The main reason we didn't want it in the house was that its poop was large and gooey.

We first set out glue traps made for mice and rats. Nothing happened. If anything, this only encouraged the wood slave, which we deduced must be female because we began noticing small carbon copies. I had mixed feelings about trying to assassinate the wood slave because they ate insects, and we had plenty.

Little by little, starting with my vacations with Ed before we bought our house, I met the Montserratians with whom he became acquainted on his work trip. One was Sharon Jones, who gave him a place to stay in her spare bedroom while he was helping repair the porch of the Methodist church's parsonage. She had a small son, Medford, who was about five years old and so shy he couldn't look Ed in the face. She invited the two of us to stay with her again when we had our "proper vacation." Sharon lived in Bethel Village "up the hill" from Spanish Point. The residents were mostly Montserratian.

Her firm invitation came in a strange way—during an amateur radio communication several months later with Tony James, a Montserratian "ham" whom Ed met in the aftermath of the hurricane. Tony wanted to know, "When are you coming home?" This was quite touching, as Ed was in love with the island and desperately wanted to see it again and to take me along so I could see it, too.

At the end of the work trip, Sharon had invited him to come again sometime and bring his wife, Ed told Tony. Without another word, Tony excused himself from the radio conversation and put in a call to her. When he returned, he said, "Sharon wants to know when you're coming home." We bought airplane tickets the next day.

(Tony James received the BEM—British Empire Medal—from Queen Elizabeth for his unceasing efforts to tell the world about the damage and loss of life Hurricane Hugo had caused.)

Many of the men and women on the Indiana work team were paired up with willing members of the Bethel Methodist Church, a stone structure with a spire, vaulted ceilings, no glass in the windows and an outhouse out back. Sharon, who had worked at one of the Plymouth banks since she was 18 years old, was a member of that church, which was a bit "down the hill" from her house.

2
GETTING THERE

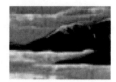

Traveling to Montserrat was not for anyone uncomfortable with airports and shuttles, lots of airports and shuttles. This, we found out on our very first trip as vacationers. To get there from our home in Indianapolis, we had to fly either north to Chicago and then back over Indianapolis on our way to Miami, or we had to first fly to Nashville, Tennessee, and make connections there for Miami or for San Juan, Puerto Rico. From Miami or San Juan, we flew to Antigua, which is still 27 miles from Montserrat. The last hop was via a small plane because the ferry that used to ply back and forth between Antigua and Montserrat had gone out of business.

Inside the Antigua airport, long lines of weary travelers trudged forward to the desks of surly immigration agents, who seemed not to care that connections missed meant holidays ruined. After negotiating the line, travelers hurried to an area not 30 yards away to find their luggage, which was trucked there from the various planes flying in and then placed ever-so-slowly on a single conveyer. Ominously, there was a large pile of unclaimed bags in one corner, much of it dented and some with the contents spilling out.

On our first trip to the island, we arrived at the counter of LIAT (Leeward Island Air Transport), which made the connecting runs to Montserrat and other islands, and received the bad news. The 7:30 p.m. flight, the last of the day, had been cancelled. Why? "Because," said the clerk in an offhand tone, "the wind is blowing too hard."

So we would have to spend the night on Antigua, not knowing what she meant by "The wind is blowing too hard." In retrospect, I'm glad we had to wait. To land on the Montserrat runway from the north, which was the usual way since it was into the prevailing wind, the pilot had to fly straight toward a seaside cliff but then, at the last minute before setting down, make a sharp turn to the left. The plane was literally poised above the crashing surf seconds before bouncing along the asphalt runway toward the terminal. Too much wind didn't sound like a very good idea for that kind of flying.

On the way to the motel on Antigua, I carried a baby on my lap, while her mama was busy with parcels. Our room had one towel, one washcloth and a ceiling fan, but no air conditioning. We were still wearing jeans and long-sleeved shirts, uniform of the north in November. The airport wasn't air conditioned either, so we were hot.

I noticed something important. The family eating a picnic dinner at the motel was black. The baby I'd held was black. His mama was black. The desk clerk was black. The waitress was black. And we were white. No one seemed to notice but me. And we soon learned that race doesn't much matter, although on some islands, we have heard, there is tension between blacks and whites. We didn't notice it on Antigua and certainly not on Montserrat. One reason: The races in the Caribbean have been mingling and interbreeding for generations. The people come in all colors along a continuum, from mahogany or ebony to pale white and everything in between.

Although the motel management promised to awaken us at 5 a.m., in time to make our flight to Montserrat, somebody forgot. At 5:15 a.m., the taxi driver banged on our door. We threw on jeans, tucked in the T-shirts we'd slept in, zipped up our suitcases, combed our hair and were ready to go.

Other passengers already in the taxi van had brought so many boxes and suitcases the driver couldn't close the rear door. It flapped against a stack of boxes as he drove the five minutes to the airport.

It was barely light when the plane landed on Montserrat. I didn't notice the cliff the pilot had to skirt. Just as well. In a few minutes, we were standing on the sidewalk outside the terminal, trying to decide whether to eat some kind of breakfast in the airport or immediately get a taxi to Sharon's house. Just then, a man rushed up to us, "Hello, Ed," he said. Ed immediately recognized Caleb Payne, his crew chief from the Hurricane Hugo building trip. Caleb said he'd just put his wife on the plane on which we'd come in; she was going for an appointment with her ophthalmologist on Antigua.

He somehow knew we were going to Sharon's and volunteered to take us there. We said, though, that we'd decided to eat breakfast at the airport so as not to bother her. He said he'd be glad to wait.

Meanwhile, our bags sat at the curb. I guess we acted nervous about them, because another man standing near us said, "Not to worry, mon. This is Montserrat." When we had eaten inside the terminal, we discovered that Caleb had put our bags in his car.

3
LIFE CHANGES

After our month-long try-out period on the island was up the end of April, 1992, I returned to work at *The Star*, but the island was always in the back of my mind. Retirement at age 65 would be in only seven years, after all. But in poring over my employer's handbook for employees, I discovered that I could start drawing on my pension right away because of the length of my tenure. All along, Ed was considered my dependent for purposes of health insurance, and his status could continue.

We had already determined that when the time came Ed could continue to work, providing direct service for his life and health insurance clients while we were in Indianapolis for the summer and then via phone and fax from Montserrat. We were sure we could live on one income until Social Security kicked in, although it might be tight.

The call of the island became stronger and stronger as the days of that summer went by. Ed and I talked and talked and then made a huge decision. Succumbing to the call of the tropics, I wrote a letter of resignation as of the middle of September, 1992, and Ed and I made plans to fly south before Christmas—along with our Labrador Retriever, Wishard, and Sunny, our orange cat.

It was such a right decision. Sitting on our porch and seeing lights on Antigua 27 miles away and, with binoculars, on Guadeloupe 40 miles away was enough to lower our blood pressure right down. We had found Eden for sure.

As the weeks went by, we learned more and more about our chosen island, including some of the disasters it had undergone before Hurricane Hugo. This knowledge was principally from a book we found in our living room's bookcase, *Montserrat West Indies: a Chronological History* by Marion M. Wheeler and published by the Montserrat National Trust in 1988. The book had gotten wet in Hurricane Hugo and smelled musty and that had an appropriateness of its own.

Here are some of the disasters:

1667 - hurricane
1670 - hurricane
1672 - earthquake
1681 - two hurricanes
1689 - earthquake
1707 - hurricane
1773 - hurricane
1833 - earthquake
1835 - hurricane
1843 - earthquake
1899 - hurricane
1924 - hurricane
1928 - hurricane
1933-35 - earthquakes
1960 - hurricane
1960s - earthquakes
1974 - earthquake

I would add: 1989 - Hurricane Hugo.

Whoa, that was a lot of disasters. But, truthfully, we didn't pay much attention to these findings. That was then; this was now. And we were very much in the "now."

During the swarms of earthquakes in the 1930s and 1960s, villagers became so frightened they refused to sleep in their houses. Instead, they pitched tents in their gardens. That was deemed safer.

The first winter on the island we put in a garden of our own. A horticulture expert we met told us a bit about the history of the island's economy, which revolved around agriculture, although what was planted changed. Before the age of fertilizers, organic farming enabled the land to produce three crops simultaneously: on terraces, which were prepared by hand. Perhaps that meant carrots could grow on a hill, sugar cane in the furrow and corn on the next hill. On the off year, a certain kind of bean was planted, and the plants were plowed under to replenish the soil, he said.

In our neighborhood, we could still see terraces left over from this long-ago planting. Of course, grass had by this time taken over everything. Slaves did all this back-breaking labor until 1834 when slavery was abolished on the island. It was no wonder, perhaps, why most Montserratian young people wanted nothing to do with farming. Their refusal, and their migration to countries with better job prospects, created a big self-sufficiency problem. It was said that one of the island's most important exports was its young adults.

Spanish Point had many infrastructure problems, which we at first thought were due to the last hurricane. But while taking a walk early in our tenure as homeowners, we met a couple driving back and forth on dirt roads looking for a water pipe break. They said the men who planned Spanish Point, hoping it would become a much-desired community of Canadian retirees, had used thin-walled (and cheap) PVC for the water pipes, and any little thing, like a farmer's attempt to stake a cow, produced a geyser, a loss of water pressure and then a lack of water altogether.

Since it was warm all the time, the pipes were buried just under the surface of the ground. The couple introduced themselves as Karl and Mary Jane Lindl and warned us about the dreaded manchineel tree, which, if touched, would result in a rash like poison ivy. It had fruit that looked like small apples, and those, too, were poison. Karl showed us what the leaves looked like before driving off. They were shiny with a prominent mid-rib.

So all was not Eden-like on Montserrat after all. But never mind. We loved the warm breezes and our friends. And we were having a wonderful time.

A major milestone in our home ownership came when the woman who worked for our lawyer in Plymouth called to say our land-holding license and title were ready to be picked up. Landholding licenses had been a problem for some who wanted to buy property on the island, we learned. This was especially true in Spanish Point, the developers of which sold lots to sun-starved Canadians at so much per month. Many Canadians attended informational meetings after seeing newspaper advertisements depicting a glamorous Caribbean life. They ended up buying land.

Some who bought made monthly payments for a while and then, deciding they were never going to build a house, stopped paying. After a time, the developer simply resold the lots, never telling the unsuspecting purchaser that the title wasn't clear. By 1992, it was not at all uncommon for a new purchaser's land-holding license to be held up for months or even, in some cases, years, while ownership was straightened out.

Meanwhile, the subdivision gave testimony to the developers' failed dreams. A motel in ruins down by the ocean was meant to be a conference center. A depression in the ground and cracked plumbing pipes were all that remained of the conference center's swimming pool. Goats wandered in and out of the cabins, which were never used. Some had no windows and no roofs, maybe because of Hurricane Hugo. On the main road was a stone entrance, remnant of the developers' attempts to build a grand retreat.

An old map of the area showed a shopping center and churches, not one of which was ever built.

4
DOG AND CAT, OH MY

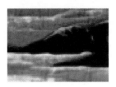

Traveling with pets wasn't simple. First off, we had to charter a plane for the last leg of our journey to Montserrat because LIAT wouldn't allow pets into Antigua until they had been in quarantine six months in England. But there was a way to get around this "no animals into Antigua rule."

If a pet-owner contacted Antigua's chief veterinarian and made arrangements, he would meet pet owners and their pets at the airport and, for US $50 per pet, he would allow everyone to pass through, provided they got off the plane that brought them to Antigua and climbed immediately onto a charter.

This was a bribe, of course, but expats who traveled to Montserrat for the winter with pets knew how the game was played. No fork over the money, no passage. That's what it boiled down to.

Nancy Stewart and her husband Melvin, Canadian neighbors of ours in Spanish Point, said they were usually able to find someone in the Antigua airport willing to split the cost of the charter. The price in the early 1990s for the 15-minute ride to Montserrat was close to $300 US dollars. Going back north required the same procedure in reverse.

There were no straight-through connections from Indianapolis, which made us nervous, as the animals were checked straight through to Miami, deemed "luggage," but all of us had our first stop in Nashville. There, we had to change planes. The cost of the first and every subsequent leg of the trip was $50 per pet.

Our first winter on the island, we took with us a very large dog cage and a regulation-size cat carrier plus three large suitcases, a 90-pound box of miscellaneous supplies from the list we'd made, two carry-ons and two small backpacks. We didn't see Sunny and Wishard in Nashville and worried that they would not make the switch, but indeed they showed up in Miami, where we would spend the night. Although we had to wait curbside for half an hour with luggage and pets in their cages, the shuttle did at last arrive to take us to our hotel. It was the only accommodation our travel agent could find that was both close to the Miami airport and would take animals.

Wishard was most appreciative, when let out of his cage, to find a grassy spot. The cat was somewhat more of a problem. Sunny had been incarcerated since very early that morning, but, cats being cats, he had not relieved himself. We had hoped to entice him to, even in a strange hotel room, by bringing along a plastic bag of kitty litter and a disposable aluminum cake pan. We set this up in the bathroom of our room and put the cat into it. He looked at us disdainfully and climbed out.

What to do? Surely poor Sunny must be in pain, we thought. What if he exploded, spraying urine all over our suite? We must take drastic action. Ed, ever the solution finder, hit upon a plan: he himself would pee into the pan. He figured that any self-respecting male cat would have to leave a calling card to show this interloper who was boss. That was the theory anyway.

When we put Sunny into the pan again, I expected a miracle. But Sunny sniffed, climbed out and circled the pan. We retreated to just out of sight around a corner, to a spot where we could still peek in and see what was going on in the maroon-tiled bathroom. He sniffed some more—and then, he climbed into the pan. What a good boy.

As a reward for our two furry friends, Ed produced dog and cat food from other plastic bags in his carry-on and put it into the paper bowls he'd also brought. Other bowls, plastic-coated, were for drinking water. We imagined that both Sunny and Wishard would be nervous about their strange surroundings, so much so that they would go crazy if we left them long enough to have dinner at a nearby restaurant. We therefore planned to call out for pizza. But when we looked into the living area a few minutes later and saw Wishard asleep in his cage and Sunny perched on the back of the sofa with his eyes closed, we opted for dinner away. When we returned, they were both still asleep.

The next morning, we got up at 5 a.m., even though our plane didn't leave until 9 a.m., had a quick breakfast and loaded onto the hotel's airport shuttle. It was a good thing we decided to go early.

Because of the Antigua laws which forbade animals from entering the country unless first quarantined for six months, the computer for the airline on which we were traveling from Miami to Antigua would not write up the paperwork for Sunny and Wishard.

Knowing this would be a problem, we had documents we were confident would help us get around the problem. Montserrat's winter visitors before us had paved the way —with guile, cunning, Yankee know-how and downright stubbornness. In the first place, Ed had a letter from the chief veterinarian on Antigua stating he would meet the plane, certify that the pets were in good health and pass us on through to our charter bound for Montserrat. Ed also had a letter from Montserrat's veterinarian, telling us the conditions under which pets were allowed there. In addition, we had a letter from our charter company stating that one of its planes had been hired to transport us from Antigua to Montserrat.

At long last, our ticket agent agreed that we were indeed legitimate and wrote tickets manually, circumventing the computer. By this time, we had just 1/2 hour to board our plane for San Juan, Puerto Rico, the next leg of the flight. But things had been going too well; at the gate we were told one of the pilots for our flight had not shown up on time. Would we make our connections in San Juan? Would there be time to load Sunny and Wishard onto our next plane?

The pilot eventually showed up and informed us that some of the lost time would be made up in the air. We had not seen Sunny and Wishard since 8 a.m. that morning. We were worried, especially when we arrived in San Juan with barely enough time to change gates and scurry onto the new plane, but our luck held. Both cages were lifted off the plane, as planned, in Antigua.

There was another problem, however. Dr. Noah, the chief veterinarian, hadn't arrived, although the pilot for Montserrat Airways was standing inside the terminal with a placard bearing our name. Someone placed a call to Dr. Noah. Ed had his "fee" at the ready.

Contrary to what we thought were Antigua rules, Sunny and Wishard's cages were brought into the airport terminal's baggage claim area, but our suitcases and the big box were in a pickup truck near the air strip, ready to be taken to the charter. We waited and waited. Soon the charter pilot and two young men working for him decided to move the animals out to the tarmac in readiness for boarding. But an angry-looking official, thinking we were about to take off without going through the proper procedure, informed our pilot that we would have to wait for Dr. Noah.

In a few minutes, the vet drove up in a van. Wearing a suit and a baseball cap, he told us he'd just been to a funeral. We expected him to inspect our pets and declare them fit, but he only peered into Sunny's cage and said, "Oh, a cat. He's asleep." Then he glanced at the dog. And that was that. Well, not quite. After an awkward pause, Ed handed over the $100, and we followed the cages out to our charter plane.

Sixteen minutes later, we landed on Montserrat, where both Vic Henry, our realtor, and a taxi driver were waiting. After clearing customs, we were informed we would have to wait until Montserrat's veterinarian came to check over our animals. So we settled down to wait again, this time on the sidewalk outside the terminal, surrounded by luggage and cages. We were concerned that neither pet had, apparently, been "watered" since 7 or 8 a.m. when we had put them into their cages, but both were sitting quietly and didn't even seem nervous.

The Montserratian vet arrived in his Range Rover, okayed Sunny and Wishard and told us he would visit us at home on Tuesday for a more thorough examination. In the meantime, the pets were to be quarantined on our property. By this time, it was nearly 5 p.m.

5
SETTLING IN

Every day we learned new things about the island, island life and customs and managing a house and grounds in the tropics.

We found out that the sputtering flame which could come while we were cooking meant that the LP gas tank out by the garage was running out, and we would have to switch to the spare tank. Unfortunately, when this first occurred, the spare was completely empty, a fact Tolbert, the previous owner, hadn't told us. Through a phone call to the gas company, we learned that in order to have propane delivered the following Thursday, the regular delivery day in our subdivision, you had to call the Drayton Gas Company by Friday of the preceding week. If we ran out of gas on a Tuesday and made a request, the person who answered the phone might have insinuated that you should have known better. A neighbor with a spare, picnic-size tank bailed us out.

When I asked earlier what people did with their garbage—assuming it would surely be picked up —I was told you put your trash in plastic bags and take it, either in your car or on foot, to the dump enclosure up the hill on the road going into town. This dump, which wasn't covered, was about two blocks from our house. We used our car for this chore.

The dump enclosure was located across the street from the clinic where people in the East went for blood pressure checks and treatment for colds, cuts and scrapes. Also on that corner was a big, round trough so villagers could bring their animals for a drink and children from homes without running water could take a bath before bedtime.

Eventually, trucks from the department of public works came to clean out the dump and carried what was inside to the island's main dumping ground, a landfill two miles or so south of us in what was called White's Ghaut. (The word "ghaut" is pronounced "gut," and comes from an East Indian word, or so I'm told, that means "ravine.")

We had seen birds flying around this area and trained the binoculars on them to see what was going on. We could also see trucks and what looked like paper blowing in the ocean breezes.

Two neighbors we met during our first winter on the island were Mamie Owensby and her husband, William. Mamie came running one day when she heard a commotion in our yard. It turned out that three little goats had somehow crawled through a hole in our fence and were chewing on our beautiful hibiscus bushes. Mamie didn't exactly apologize, but she stated that the baby goats' mother had died a couple of weeks before. When they grew a bit bigger, she said, they wouldn't be able to slip through such a small hole in our fence.

So that was our introduction to another fact of island life: Much of the livestock was loose. Goats, particularly, would eat anything and everything. If you cared about your landscaping, you had a sturdy fence and a gate you kept shut. Mamie showed me a place in our front gate where she and William had laced string to keep the goats out.

We were told more than once that animals on the island were a mark of worth—the larger the herd, the greater the master's worth. Those who kept animals didn't necessarily sell them, but they could if they needed cash. Cows, sheep and goats were an investment, rather like shares of Procter and Gamble or General Motors. Anybody who owned 400 sheep or goats was a powerful man or woman indeed.

During our first conversation with Mamie, she said she and William were born on Montserrat, but in different parts of the island and didn't know each other until they met in England where they had gone to work. He was a maintenance man in a factory, and she was a free-lance seamstress and caterer, specializing in weddings. I could hardly fathom how people lived on a 39 1/2 square mile island the size of Montserrat and didn't know each other. But then western expats and eastern expats didn't know each other either.

We cleaned up Paradise East little by little, commensurate with our energy and the sun. Since we sat on the porch a lot looking at the ocean and at Antigua, I made cleaning up the porch, called a "gallery" by the Canadians, a priority. I gathered up more plastic containers and began to move the furniture so I could sweep. There was a tired-looking wooden end table against the front porch wall. When I picked it up, its legs disintegrated, and the resulting dust was blown away by the wind. Then I noticed a termite tunnel crossing the porch floor. It traveled up the decorative, concrete-block porch rail and down the other side to the ground, where it disappeared into a hibiscus bush. I made a note to contact an exterminator, not only for the termites, but also for the cockroaches. It was clear: we needed someone on a regular basis.

Soon, we developed a routine. We would get up at 5:15 a.m. so we could sit on the porch with our coffee and watch the sun come up. Then we would finish eating our breakfast before taking a tour of the back yard with a second cup of coffee to see what had sprouted or grown in the night. After this trip around the back yard, a little chopping or weeding would follow, until no later than 10 a.m. when the sun became a bit too hot and too direct for us Yankees.

Or I might spend time cleaning cabinets or shelves. One morning, I concentrated on the "entertainment center," from which I threw away a broken thermometer, an antique pitcher that had been dropped and poorly repaired and a cracked punchbowl.

Fresh from the shower, on many mornings, we drove into town and ran errands. Sometimes, we ate lunch there, sometimes not. We tried to make it a rule not to work after lunch. After all, we were supposed to be on vacation. Vic Henry, the real estate agent and our neighbor, often said, "You didn't come down here to kill yourself." We paid attention.

The need to cool off after some exertion was a good excuse to sit on the porch and just look at our surroundings. We especially loved to watch the lambs cavorting in a pasture across the street. Often, they would be walking along and suddenly jump straight up, seemingly for no reason except pure joy. When they got tired and hungry and found their mother for a snack, we would turn our attention to the kingbird that had built a nest on a nearby phone pole and dive-bombed any bird that flew too close.

It was easy to spend an hour in these pursuits, and somehow we didn't think the time was being wasted.

As the sun beat straight down from 10 a.m. to 2 p.m. and since we had been warned and warned about skin cancer, we didn't go swimming until after 2. Between lunch and our daily swim, Ed would get on the air with his amateur radio and talk to people all over the world, including such exotic places as the Chagos Islands and Antarctica.

One of our activities that first winter was to visit Tony James, the amateur radio friend, who lived on the Westside in a village high up above the coastline. Ed apologized to Tony for failure to fix a mistake in a computer program for printing amateur radio licenses. Tony dispensed all the licenses on the island, and Ed's program, meant to make life easier by creating a one-page template, was causing one sentence to slop over onto a page two.

Ed referred to his failure as a "problem" whereupon Tony reminded him, "It's not a problem. It's just a situation." A typically Montserratian point of view and one we tried to remember. There really weren't many "problems."

I tried to swim laps in our pool at least every other day after 2 p.m. I loved to watch palm fronds gently swaying in the trade winds as I did the backstroke to and fro in our pool, definitely a high spot of the day. Despite the sun and the location 17 degrees from the Equator, however, we discovered, to our surprise, that 80 degrees with a stiff breeze was a bit too chilly for swimming. The next day would be calmer. We counted on that.

Transplanted Americans, Brits and Canadians who lived on the island full-time told us they didn't swim from late November until, perhaps, early March. Gladys Henry, Vic's wife, said the extremely windy and chilly air occurred routinely during the Montserrat winter. Sometimes, she said, the thermometer went down to 68 degrees at night. The health department then would put out an urgent plea for the donation of blankets because poor old people were suffering. Nobody had a furnace. And many closed their windows with ill-fitting wooden shutters rather than glass.

About 5 p.m., give or take a little, an army of tree frogs tuned up from their perches in the many hibiscus bushes ringing our yard. This was the frogs' signal to all who heard that the daylight hours would soon end. In the tropics, close to the equator where days and nights are equal, sunset is early when compared to the times we were used to in the Midwestern United States. On Montserrat, there were no long summer evenings of daylight. The days were nearly the same length, winter and summer.

At this point in our living on Montserrat, we thought growing anything in our garden would be easy, given the lushness of some gardens we had seen. We thought every seed germinated, and the afternoon rains were sufficient for plant growth. We noticed that Mamie had an avocado growing in her garden, and I thought to myself how easy it would be to buy an avocado at the supermarket and plant the seed in the yard, and it would grow and thrive and bear bushels of avocados. It didn't happen.

We were nearly as inept dealing with the coconuts, which we had in abundance. Ed had knocked down two coconuts with the handle of our pool skimmer, but smashing one with a concrete block failed to open it. In a dashing effort reminiscent of the "Charge of the Light Brigade," he fell upon the coconut with a pick and thus cracked the hull. This turned out to be overkill, as coconut milk spilled out on the ground, and what was left of the meat was smashed into small pieces, smaller than we'd hoped for.

I tried to separate husk from coconut meat with a hammer and managed to get enough useful to grate a cupful, which was called for in a cookie recipe I'd found. "Going native" meant we didn't eat dinner that night until 7:30 p.m.

Early one morning, Ed announced that he was going to mend the fence down in the ghaut behind our house so that no goat of any size could find its way in. He had tromped through waist-high grass the day before and thought he had found a hole. It was hot and steamy on the ghaut side of the fence, but Ed wore long pants anyway. There might be things there that would poke him while he worked, and I told him there was no way he was going to swing a cutlass (machete) wearing shorts. There was a saying on the island that there is nothing more dangerous than a white man with a cutlass.

Our insect invasions were not only of cockroaches; they were of what we grew to call the "ibb's," or "itty, bitty bugs." They looked like tiny flies, but they could easily pass through our window screens and were attracted to light. When the air was still after dark, or when the breeze came off the center of the island rather than the coast, it was prudent to close the windows, find a lantern or a flashlight and turn off the lights.

The invasion would start with only a few of the ibb's, but if the precautions weren't taken, there would be literally thousands. They didn't bite or sting. They just flew in through the screens, hovered around the lamps or the TV set and then died. An invasion would be over in about an hour.

The first time we experienced the little bugs, I told Sharon that

I had just cleaned that day and then had to run the vacuum sweeper again. She said these bugs only visited clean houses. At first, I thought she was serious.

Nancy Stewart, one of our Canadian neighbors, knew a lot about gardening. In fact, she could grow anything , and I often consulted her about matters horticultural. Vic Henry told us the cashew tree in our backyard had termites and ought to be cut down. Nancy, though, said our exterminator could deal with the problem. I had no idea the tree in question was a cashew. I had no idea either that termites would invade living trees and that they could only be kept at bay, never eliminated, not in the tropics.

Nancy showed us that we had a "paw-paw," as they were called on Montserrat, just over the fence. We Hoosiers would call the tall, woody plant a papaya. I am so used to calling the luscious fruit a paw-paw now that even today I can't break the habit. This is the story of the paw-paw: here today and gone tomorrow. A plant could keep growing taller and producing fruit, and then, for no apparent reason, fall over dead. Paw-paw plants can break your heart, Nancy said.

Angie, Sharon's sister, was also a plant expert. She told me that the almost leafless tree behind our house was either a lemon, orange or grapefruit. She couldn't tell which. But, she said, its loss of leaves and blackened branches were the result of insects. It needed to be pruned back and sprayed.

Angie pointed out a soursop tree with a large fruit on it. Such trees usually grow in the shade of a much bigger tree, she said, and ours was no exception. It was growing under our cashew tree. The soursop fruit is an ugly, green, misshapen glob with spines, but peeled, mashed and run through a sieve, it supposedly "makes a lovely drink," or so Angie said.

We were fascinated with the stories of how our neighbors had found Montserrat, so many miles away from the US and Canada— and of course, Britain. We could understand how the Brits knew about it. After all, they owned it.

The longer we lived in Spanish Point, which was, in fact, a semi-arid slope overlooking the airport, we learned more and more about the mainly Canadians who lived there. At a dinner at neighbor Helen Adams', for example, we learned that Karl, who, with his wife Mary Jane, spent summers in a cabin in the woods near Toronto, came to the island in the early '70s to see lots advertised by the Canadian developers.

They had been coming to Montserrat for 12 years, Mary Jane said, sipping a drink the principal ingredient of which was sour sop from her yard. She had liquefied the sour sop in her blender, added milk and then rum—and brought a large bottle to the party to share. Helen, not knowing Mary Jane already had added rum, put in some more.

The dinner menu was laid-back like the general lifestyle, and based on whatever was available in the grocery stores downtown in Plymouth. Helen served manicotti stuffed with cheese and covered before baking with bottled spaghetti sauce, a carrot and raisin salad, celery sticks (a real find), deviled eggs, sliced tomatoes from her garden and fruitcake (another real find, according to Montserrat expats more experienced than I).

6
FOOD, GLORIOUS FOOD

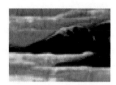

One of the lovable characters we met early during our one-month, try-out period was Katy Connor, the ve-ge-TAY-bull lady. When we first saw her, she was walking past our gate carrying satchels of fruits and vegetables. She wore an old felt hat squashed down on her head, covering grizzled, gray pigtails. Mr. Tolbert, she said, had brought her down to Spanish Point from her house in the village called Harris' because another neighbor of ours, a Mr. Fleming, needed bananas. Mr. Tolbert, she said, "was one of my best customers." I took this as a hint that I should be the same.

The Montserrat habit of making town names possessive, as in Harris', probably came from slave times when the acres where the town sprang up were owned by a Mr. Harris. There were also the villages of Tuitt's, Dyer's and Gerald's on the island. No Montserratian I asked seemed to know how the towns got their names.

During that earliest period, we didn't know Tolbert was still on the island. He'd not told us, and the bill of sale gave us possession on April 1. Katy said he planned to stay on Montserrat with a friend until May 10, when the weather was warmer up north. We felt bad, not knowing what his plans were, but we were already in the house and had started cleaning it up. It needed a lot of cleaning.

On the day Tolbert finally did leave the island, Katy walked down from her house in Harris' to sell vegetables, but also to tell him goodbye. We didn't need any produce, but we did offer her a drink of water and a ride home, both of which she accepted.

Sitting on the porch to have her drink, she told us how she used to bring three of her children down to Spanish Point to help her carry produce. Her home was at least two miles up the hill—or the mountain, if you will—from us. She said her children were all grown up with their own lives to live. Her doctor didn't want her carrying so much, but, she said, she didn't pay attention.

One of the things she told us that day was her "Hugo story." Over the years we wintered on the island, we heard a lot of them, but hers was probably the most dramatic. Knowing that her wooden shack might not be safe during the worst of the storm, she took Mark, a mentally challenged son, and went to the home of a friend, whose wooden house had a concrete-block addition.

As she was walking toward her neighborhood when the storm abated, someone told her that her house had blown away and could be found "in de ghaut," down the hill from its previous spot. When she checked to see for herself, she discovered that the roof had caved in around the foundation before the rest blew away, along with all her belongings, which were strewn around on the ground "all mucked up."

The government saw to it that she received what was known as a "Hugo House," a pre-fabricated, two-room cabin made of treated lumber to ward off termites. The island was full of these little houses, which were set onto concrete blocks and could be moved at almost a moment's notice.

It wasn't unusual to see Katy hurrying down the hill hefting a satchel bulging with paw-paws, green peppers and cabbage in each hand while balancing a metal basin of bananas on her head. I asked Katy how she was able to carry things on her head, and she showed me how she coiled a rag and placed it on top of her ever-present hat. The coil was called a "wad," and it helped her balance a pan or basket. The whole operation came so easily for her that she could hardly explain it. She said young people no longer want to learn how to use their heads in such a way. It was up to young people, she insisted, to carry on the island's traditions and not let them die.

She told us Tolbert would be leaving the airport at 2 p.m. that day, and we decided to take him the Bible and the photographs of him and his wife that we had found while cleaning out the drawer of a tea wagon in our dining room. (When I opened the drawer, a lizard had hopped out, scaring me half to death.) Several of the neighbors who had known Tolbert for years also drove down for an airport send-off. Someone brought a flower for his buttonhole. It was a happy occasion only on the surface, as the neighbors no doubt wondered if they would ever see him again.

That's the way it is with winter, or summer, friendships when you're old. A few months away can mean a change in health or a quick death, and a casual goodbye can be forever. This can be true for younger people, too, but they either prefer not to think about the possibility of permanent separation or don't believe it will happen. Old people know, and that makes parting unusually sad.

We heard later that when Tolbert returned to Canada, his son helped him move to a nursing home, where he died two months later. I heard more than once, both from indigenous Montserratians and from expatriates, that leaving the island broke his heart.

Katy became very important in our lives because the supply of produce in the markets in Plymouth was unreliable. So we purchased from her every two or three days. Sometimes, she would phone us to say what she had available. Sometimes, she just appeared at our gate. Sometimes, we phoned her to place an order.

On the way to the beach to go swimming one day, we stopped off at Katy's house to pick up the bananas she said, in an early-morning phone conversation, she was saving for us. When I walked down the road that used to go by the front of her house until erosion changed the hillside, I saw her on my left cutting the tops from onions. As she did not have running water in her house, she had also been washing clothes in a bucket outside. The clean laundry hung on a rope she had stretched between two trees at the top of the cliff.

Her personal life was a soap opera, as I discovered almost every time I went to her house to pick up our vegetables and fruits. On this day, I looked to my right as I approached her because I sensed movement in my peripheral vision. An old man leaned out of the window of a shack not five feet away from hers, looking at me but not saying anything. Who was that? I didn't ask at that time, but quizzed Mamie Owensby about it later.

That was Katy's husband, Mamie said. He and Katy no longer lived together because he was a wife beater. Because she was ultra religious, she believed everything her minister said about the sanctity of marriage, no matter what. So she didn't divorce him. Several days later, when we weren't home, Katy placed a plastic bag of green beans, three bananas and a paw-paw on our porch, then stopped by later in the day for her money. She said she had to go home to cook for the family before attending a tent revival meeting in Plymouth. I said,

"Oh, you're cooking for yourself and Mark?"

Katy said, "No, for my husband and Nigel (another son), too." I thought her husband only lived in the shack next door to her, and providing living quarters constituted the extent of their relationship. Katy said he had asked her to cook for him and promised to pay for the food. Although she tried earlier to get a lawyer to help her move the husband off her property, both men came from the same village on the island. So the lawyer "didn't do nothing."

Another lawyer whose services she sought sent her husband a letter, telling him he'd be evicted from the property if his behavior was untoward in any way. Katy said he had "been better since then," meaning he didn't hit her and yelled at her less.

Life around her corner of Harris' tended to be chaotic and not just because of the presence of her husband. As we were buying vegetables from her one day, we heard a man yelling from down the road near her house. Looking in the direction of the noise, we saw a gray-haired man, arm raised and obviously directing his venom at us. "Is he drunk?" I asked Katy. "Always," she said. "He is a raving lu-NA-TIC."

We were told later that the man, called Hoagie Darnell, sometimes fell asleep in the road, which didn't get all that much traffic. We were advised to watch out when we drove through his neighborhood, lest we round a curve and find him sprawled out on the warm pavement.

It wasn't long before we heard from Katy that Darnell had acted up again. He went into town and bought a bottle of brandy, which he began, methodically, to drink. Soon, she said, he started shouting, "Who did it? Who did it? Who did it?"

I told her to turn her radio up loud so she couldn't hear the ruckus. "I used to tape record him," she said.

"Who did you play the tapes for?" I asked.

"Up in the village. For fun," Katy said, amid peals of laughter.

Many times, we stopped off at Katy's on our way into town. I was surprised on one occasion to see her making a pile of coconut husks and setting them on fire. With the help of Mark, she laid a large snake, stunned but not dead, atop the pyre. "This is what we do," she said, very solemnly. "This is what we do." When the flames, fueled, I think, by kerosene, were high, and the snake, which was about four feet long, stopped wiggling, she turned her attention to us.

I knew that Montserratians hated almost all wild animals, thinking them competitors, no doubt, in the raising of food for humans, but had never seen such vehemence in dispatching one of them. Could there be something fiercely biblical about killing the snake, the beast that tempted Eve?

When paying her for the paw-paws, cucumbers, green beans and bananas I had ordered, I noticed that she had a "coalpot" set up in the middle of what had been the road behind her house, and it was steaming. The coalpot was a charcoal cooker many poor people who didn't have stoves used. Was Katy planning on cooking the snake? I didn't think so, but I asked her what was cooking for dinner. "Tripe soup," she said, slurping spit through her missing front teeth.

"Where did you get the tripe?" I asked.

She grinned that snaggle-toothed, happy grin I liked so much. "I have my supplier," she said.

Her life seemed to be happy, then unhappy in a continuing spiral that was mainly downward. When we drove to Katy's house sometime later to deliver prints we had taken of her carrying a large box on her head, she ran down her driveway to greet us. I noticed that her husband was out in front of the house with another man, talking loudly. She saw that I noticed and immediately burst into tears. Her husband had been calling her bad names all day, she said. This had been going on for years, ever since they married in the 1960s. She was tired of her miserable life.

In recent weeks, she said, she had contacted another attorney and asked him to write a letter ordering her husband to stop calling her names. That didn't work, she said. She asked her minister to talk to her husband, but that only made things worse. Her husband was at his worst when he was drinking, which was most of the time when he wasn't working. He had a job as foreman for the garbage collectors on the island.

At this point, Katy said, she was at the end of her rope. I became alarmed because she seemed depressed, and I tried exploring options with her. I wondered if she could contact Family Life Services, the island's counseling agency. She agreed to do that, and we said we would pick her up and take her to their office.

When we arrived at home, Ed suggested that we call Lucy Evans, a nurse retired from duty many years in England, to ask her advice. Lucy told us that Family Life Services' goal was to keep families together, which might not be appropriate in Katy's case.

The problems with her husband seemed to subside slowly, but

that didn't make her life totally pleasant. She still had trouble paying her bills. A couple of times, she called and asked us to stop by her house as we went into town and pick up money with which to pay a bill for her. Invariably, she gave us a plastic bag full of coins. When money was especially tight and a bill needed to be paid, she would phone us to see if we needed green beans or lettuce or bananas. She never told us that a bill was due, but we guessed and always tried to help her out.

Somewhat later, Katy phoned us to ask another favor: Would we mind taking a picture of her? She offered no details. Of course, we were glad to do so and made a date for that very afternoon. When we arrived, she jumped out from behind a bush. If I had seen her on the streets of Plymouth, I wouldn't have known her. Instead of wearing her usual mismatched hand-me-downs, little braids and a bashed-up hat, she was wearing a peach-colored dress with long lace sleeves and lace appliqués on the skirt; an enormous garden hat with a semi-transparent brim and a beaded crown; white, high-heeled shoes; white hose; a salt-and-pepper wig with tight curls, and a pair of reading glasses slightly askew on her nose.

We didn't mean to pry, but I couldn't pass up the chance to ask her what the occasion was going to be. It turned out that she had already attended a wedding wearing the dress, which her sister had sent her from St. John, Virgin Islands. Katy had a friend take a picture of her in the dress just after the wedding, but, later, he was unable to find the film.

The way the outfit arrived on Montserrat showed the ingenuity of the people in obtaining the things they wanted. Some youths from her church were going to St. John, so she gave them her sister's phone number and asked them to make contact, which they did. The sister sent the dress down with the kids when they returned to Montserrat.

7
SHOPPING

Every walk around our house or garden brought out the shopping list. At first, we were driving into town nearly every day. The list could be as diverse as a plug for the bathtub, some shelf paper, potholders and a magic marker. As always, a shopping trip meant poking into several stores before we could find what we needed. For example, there were six hardware stores, and you could buy only part of your list in any one of them. A keyhole saw might be available in one store, but not the blades.

As time went on, we were told that if you saw something you thought you might need in the future, you should buy it right then. When you really needed the item, the chances were good it wouldn't be available. And expect to find what you were looking for in peculiar places. The shoe shop sold transformers, necessary to make appliances compatible with 220-volt service. The equivalent of the island's Radio Shack carried shoes. I found a tire gauge in a dry goods store that sold mostly bed and bath linens and ladies' underwear.

I began making a list of what store carried what. I learned that Essie's, an all-purpose store with a grumpy proprietor, had sheets, plastic dishes, blankets, hair care products, ladies' underwear, clothespins and crochet cotton. I noted that the Lincoln Pharmacy sold zippers, buttons, lipstick, embroidery floss and flea powder.

While enjoying a brownie and tea at a new snack shop in Plymouth, we met a tourist couple who wanted to know where they could buy fresh fish on the island. I had to tell them that most of the fish I'd seen was hard as a rock in the freezer of Ram's Supermarket. I knew that some people did buy fresh fish somewhere, but I had never, or almost never, seen it.

The man was horrified about the state of produce in the markets. I told him the produce was brought in by local farmers primarily on Fridays and Saturdays, but that if he saw it on Tuesday, it was bound to look limp as it was not iced down. A little fresh food came in by boat from all over the Caribbean and from the USA. That, too, often was limp when it arrived.

Almost everyone had someone like Katy Connor who kept them supplied with fresh vegetables and fruits, I said, or they raised produce themselves for personal consumption. Privately, I thought that if he were to become an islander, he would have to get over being horrified about the looks of the imported celery in Ram's and just quietly do without when the quality was low.

In addition to the frozen fish, some of the markets had either cod or mackerel dried, salted and then sealed in meal-size plastic bags. It was called, appropriately, "saltfish." I didn't deem this a desirable food to buy because it stank up the stores, more pungently than Americans and particularly landlocked Midwesterners, were used to. The good thing was that, thus preserved, the fish didn't need refrigeration and could be kept, I assumed, forever.

As time went on, I wanted to learn to cook saltfish, as it was a staple in the Montserratian diet. I found recipes in the *Montserrat Cookbook*, compiled as a fund-raiser for the Montserrat Old People's Welfare Association in 1973.

Saltfish and Reggae

Saltfish Casserole
1 pound saltfish (Or you could use any non-fishy tasting fish, such as tilapia, and skip the steps about reconstituting it. The fish should, however, be pre-cooked, perhaps by broiling, until it is done.)
   3-4 potatoes, sliced and boiled until soft
   3-4 onions, sliced
   1 can Italian-style tomatoes, drained
   1 teaspoon basil
   salt and pepper to taste
   milk
   butter and breadcrumbs
   2 hardboiled eggs, sliced

First, soak the fish in water overnight to reconstitute it. After the soaking, boil in several changes of water. Remove the meat from the bones. The bits should be small.

In a greased casserole, alternate layers of potato, fish, onions and tomatoes. Pour on a little milk, add egg slices and sprinkle with seasonings and crumbs. Dot with butter. Bake at 375 degrees about 45 minutes or until brown and heated through.

Saltfish is so well known in the Caribbean a reggae song has been written about it. Popularized by Jamaican musician Bob Marley in the 1970s, reggae is a combination of two Jamaican styles of music, but has infusions of American jazz and African music, too. It is slow, with offbeat rhythms and syncopation. Drums, bass guitar, keyboard (including sometimes the Hammond organ) and horns are used. Singing is secondary. Some lyrics are political, but not always. And it does reflect the interests and habits of the culture it comes out of.

We soon grew tired of driving to the laundromat and went looking for a washing machine to purchase. Karl Lindl told us that a place up by the hospital might have what we were looking for. The store was called Lester's Warehouse and was hard to find because there was no sign out front. Karl knew where it was because he had just purchased a microwave there for about $260 US dollars. That was quite expensive back in the '90s, but, on Montserrat, what wasn't?

Lester's Warehouse, which was located in an estate house reconstructed from slave times, was otherwise known as "Fine Furniture and Appliances," and on the day we shopped there, we were the only customers. A Roper washer was priced at $787 US dollars. (Lester's was asking $1,180 for a 16 cubic-foot Whirlpool refrigerator with no bells and whistles.)

We reminded ourselves, however, that we were spending about the equivalent of $13 US at the laundromat each week. In less than two winters, we would pay for a new washer from Lester's, even at inflated prices.

Ever on the hunt, we were told about a used machine, which had been shipped to the island from Miami only a few years before. It hadn't been used in about a year, however, because the people who owned it had decided they wouldn't be coming back to the island. It was a General Electric, no frills. Although barely used, the washer had been in a carport and thus was partially exposed to weather.

Vic Henry, who was acting as the go-between because he was in charge of looking after the house where the washer was located, told us he would call the owner and see what he could arrange. We hoped to pay $400 or less. In a few days, Nick, who worked for Vic, drove up with his truck containing our new-to-us washing machine, which the owners were willing to sell for just under $400. Ed put it in our concrete block garage and hooked it up to the garden hose.

Although we no longer had to go to the coin laundry, we still searched for various items to make our household confortable. Often we were told particular items were "finished." This meant that they were out of stock at the moment we wanted them. The finished items might be in stock again in a week or two, or never. And some things, inexplicably, were not available in the form we expected. While the island had lots of cows, pasteurized milk in a bottle or cardboard carton could not be found.

Most of the island's poor cows were so dehydrated they barely had milk enough for their calves, which nursed until they were as big as their mothers. For some reason, the supermarket was sometimes out of milk, which came in one-liter boxes, unrefrigerated, and packaged by Nestle.

A radio story about food on the island caught my attention. I learned that price controls were in effect for such things as rice, flour, sardines, tuna, mackerel, cooking oil and corn meal. Other food necessities, with luck, could be grown on the island, or so went the theory. Because of lack of storage capacity, however, Montserrat could only grow 17 acres of potatoes, which at that time, covered only 50 percent of the island's needs.

Forty percent of chicken consumed on the island was grown there, and 30 people were employed in the chicken business. The island grocery stores, even Ram's, the biggest supermarket, which tended to have items that other stores didn't, remained out of garbage bags and kitty litter for weeks. Someone told us it was possible to dry cat litter in the sun and use it again. Other cat owners had taken to digging sand along the beaches, which was supposed to be a no-no. The prohibition was really meant to keep home builders from taking truckloads of beach sand and using it to make stucco.

There was no way to tell how long various products had been on the shelves. I opened a bag of dried beans to soak one evening, thinking I would get the jump on the next day's evening meal. I discovered to my horror that many of the beans had been drilled into—or out of—by small bugs, or their predecessors, the caterpillars, which floated to the top of the soak water and even, audaciously, swam around. What should I do? Should I throw the whole lot away or salvage what I could? Because by then I had become a true islander, I opted for the second option. This I did not convey to my spouse, but surreptitiously for the rest of the evening, I repeatedly went over to the bowl and removed the recent hatches. The bean soup I made the next day tasted wonderful.

Since there were no bedspreads or comforters available in any of the stores I checked, I decided to make my own, using a cotton blanket for batting, a colorful fish print sheet on top and a plain sheet on the bottom. I had brought all these materials from the States plus yarn to tie the comforter.

I spent most of one day tying yarn on the comforter: a square knot every four inches. By the end of the process, my fingers were sore from jabbing the needle in and out of the high-thread-count fabric. I hadn't considered there might be a problem when I opted to use sheets. The end product, however, was quite pleasing, and the purple and turquoise fish considerably brightened our bedroom.

We maintained an ongoing list of things we intended to "bring down" next season. It varied from "gasket for the oven door" to "brads to fix the rattan chairs" to "plastic curtain rods" to replace the rusty ones with which the house came equipped. This list grew quite long by the end of the season, and we would always spend several days and quite a bit of money amassing everything for the next winter.

Nancy, whose husband had gone to Canada for a few weeks, called to ask Ed to fix her water heater. Ed told her she might be able to buy any needed part in town, but if not, she would have to take tepid showers and boil dish water on the stove until Melvin, her husband, returned with the necessary part in his luggage.

This was the way most repairs were made—with the cooperation of family and friends. For example, houseguests of ours brought down a new burner for Nancy's Tappan range; repair parts for it were not available on the island.

It didn't get us anywhere to be frustrated about the shopping deficiencies or the slowness of getting anything accomplished on the island. Some aspects of Caribbean life didn't change, no matter what we did, or didn't do. When we went into town with what we thought was a very straightforward errand list, we knew we wouldn't be able to accomplish everything on it. Batting 50 percent represented a good day.

On one trip into town, my errand list included: 1. Pay the car insurance premium. 2. Buy some garden gloves. 3. Buy stamps at the post office. 4. Buy a muffin tin. 5. Buy tickets for the dance competition that had been announced on the radio. 6. Buy the hair dressing I'd been using to cut down on chlorine damage from swimming. 7. Buy lettuce.

We tried in several shops to buy the muffin tin. In the most likely place, the Montserrat Stationery Center, which also had a housewares department, we were told, "We had them last week, but we had a sale and they're finished." For the dance tickets, we tried the little news kiosk, which usually had tickets for events. But the young woman who worked there told us she didn't have the tickets yet because they hadn't been printed. I went into the store where I'd always bought a particular kind of hair dressing, and the clerk said, "We don't have any, but Pauline's might." She didn't either.

When we went to buy lettuce at the garden where it was being grown hydroponically, I was told there wasn't any but "come back tomorrow." From the sales room, I could look through a window into the area where the lettuce was growing in special trays, absorbing its nutrients from the water, so I knew there was lettuce, just no lettuce in the cooler where it was kept after it was cut. And what did they have in the cooler? Green beans. I bought some.

Driving home, we picked up David Fleming, who was walking down the mountain toward Spanish Point from Harris'. He was at least two miles from home when we caught up with him. He said he had taken his car up to the service station so Rondell Cabey, the station owner, could repair it. This was the same car Fleming had driven over the cliff the previous spring, and "Rondo," as he was known, had only recently received the windshield for it.

I was sewing a wall hanging made with fabric I had bought in the States, but I needed commercial cotton for the backing. I knew I wouldn't be able to find 100 percent cotton; every cotton fabric I had seen was part polyester. I tried the three stores I knew about that carried fabric, but nobody had the right shade of purple. At Darlington's dry goods store, Mrs. Darlington told us to try "Sylvie's" for fabric and explained to us where that shop could be found. Sylvie's was across the street from Cable and Wireless, the telephone company, but wasn't marked.

Actually, there was a sign on the building which said "Patty's Hygrade," whatever that meant. There was a calico cat asleep on the counter and more fabric than I'd seen in one place anywhere on the island. And Sylvie had exactly the color fabric I needed to complete my wall hanging; it was polyester and cotton, but I had ceased caring. She also sold buttons, pots and pans and hair care products, I observed.

Usually, even a frustrating shopping expedition could be turned into a happy occasion. We'd looked all over without success for a buck saw with which to prune some trees that had grown so tall and bent over they were shedding dead leaves into our swimming pool. But then we spied an ice cream vendor, from whom we purchased two cups of guava ice cream. We carried them to the car, which we'd parked down by the pier, and sat eating as we watched little fishing boats bobbing on the waves.

A trip into town usually included a stop at Grimes' Wayside Store, which more likely than not had what we were after in the hardware department. On one occasion, Mrs. Grimes, the patrician-looking woman who, with her children, owned the store, took me aside and asked if I could help her. She said she had just been named to head the Seventh-day Adventist School and wondered if I, with my contacts in the United States, could find her some sequential textbooks kindergarten through eighth grade, particularly in spelling and reading. If possible, she said, she would like 15 copies and the teacher's manual, but the numbers weren't important.

Mrs. Grimes said she didn't care if the books were new or used, and she didn't care if the books were "culturally biased," meaning they were written for predominantly white children in a First World country. I knew what she meant. Vocabulary is vocabulary, and spelling is spelling—except for some variation between British and American. ("Color" is American; "colour" is British.) Many books on the island, she went on, were destroyed in Hurricane Hugo.

I had no idea where I would get such books in such large quantities, but I promised I would do what I could.

I wrote a teacher friend in Indianapolis to see if she had any way to assemble the books Mrs. Grimes needed for the Seventh-day Adventist School. And in a few weeks, my friend called to say she was able to get 90 books from her school system: teachers' manuals and students' books for reading and spelling, kindergarten through 8th grade. These books had been declared obsolete and soon would be thrown away.

Her find was big enough that every child in the school could have a book. The next question was how to ship the books to Montserrat as inexpensively as possible.

In the meantime, we needed to work on our perennial "situation": the yard and the pests which were devouring it. This meant we had to visit the agricultural station. That could be interesting.

Soca

Brian Cassell, an enterprising young man from the agricultural staion who was to help us with our yard problems, was also a budding singer and song writer. He had made a cassette of his Soca songs, which he asked us to buy. We said, sure, we'd buy a copy of his tape, because we admired his drive and were curious about what kind of music a guy who sold fertilizer and products to kill bugs would write. When we got the tape home, we discovered it had only two songs on the first side, and the same two songs on the other side.

Born in Trinidad and Tobago, "Soca" music is a fusion of soul and calypso with the influence of India because of the types of East Indian instruments often used. A rapid percussion beat is a strong feature.

"Arrow," a Montserratian Soca singer, recorded several albums during the 1980s and '90s. He was known internationally.

8
BUGS AND OTHER PESTS

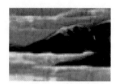

Besides the Wayside Store, another usual stop was "The Grove," the island's agriculture station. One day, we wanted to pick up some Malathion to spray our citrus trees, which had a sooty fungus and aphids. Liquid Malathion, in the 1990s, was sold in empty gin bottles with "Poison" written on a masking tape label.

The keeper of all the potions and powders to kill household pests, Brian Cassell, sat in the shade outside his office/warehouse and talked to friends while waiting for customers. From 100-pound bags, he would weigh out 10 pounds of dry fertilizer or dry pesticide and put it in a paper bag, which he didn't label. No instructions came with anything purchased this way. He liked it a lot when you bought big quantities, preferably the whole 100 pounds he had received off the container ship down at the pier.

As time went on, a chart telling what each pesticide was good for and some safety rules was tacked up on the wall of his office. But that didn't happen when we were first on the island.

The yard needed attention almost as much as the inside of the house. Ed had repaired the fence so the goats couldn't get in and eat everything. But what they hadn't chewed up was overgrown. So on one trip into town, we bought what I call "loppers" and some hand trimmers.

Since the soil looked to be rocky and not too nutritious, I thought the bushes and trees needed to be fertilized, but had not been able to find the kind and make-up that I wanted. Perhaps it wouldn't be necessary to purchase fertilizer, I thought. The pastures around our house were frequented by lots of cows, and that meant lots of cow pies.

I found some old garden gloves in the garage, a bucket and a shovel and went to work. The shovel turned out not to be helpful, but the pies were mostly dried in the sun. Picking them up with my gloved hands and tossing them into the bucket seemed to be the expedient way of gathering up my natural fertilizer.

Cow pies tended to be full of insects. This fact was not lost on other creatures; one I picked up had an enormous toad under it—shelter and dinner all in the same spot. He was quite disturbed that I had blown his cover, as he would normally be nocturnal. I gave him a wide berth, as toads on the island exuded a poisonous or at least a noxious substance, which was said to be a skin irritant to humans and possibly lethal to small dogs and cats.

I wasn't too worried about Wishard because we always watched him when we let him out to do his business, and Sunny, who had no claws, was never allowed outside.

When I brought the cow pies home, I chopped up some and worked them into the soil in the bed where I was planting a variety of spinach especially bred for the tropics. Actually, it was called a "leaf beet" or "perpetual spinach" but wasn't really spinach although it was cooked the same way. It was called "perpetual" because you could pick off the leaves, and new ones would grow. With a true spinach, you cut off the plant at ground level to harvest it, and that is that.

Late one afternoon William arrived at our front gate with a burlap sack full of banana shoots and his cutlass to plant MY banana plantation—the plantation that within a few months would feed our family and, if we were lucky, half of Spanish Point, with lovely bananas. Or so I fantasized.

William brought one plantain (cooking banana), one regular banana and a dwarf banana the taste of which I really liked. Katy called them "figs," or "figueroas." All the shoots looked exactly the same to me, and William didn't say which was which. Using his cutlass, William dug one hole down near the ghaut to the south of our property, and Ed helped him dig the other two holes in the yard near our back door. We asked if we should fertilize the shoots, which looked like peony corms, only huge. William said the earth was rich enough that I wouldn't need to do anything.

William had timed his arrival to plant, he said, "by the moon, two days after the first quarter." This was a serious thing and had to be strictly adhered to. He said all this without even the hint of a smile, so I didn't smile either.

When this project was finished, Ed and I drove William up the mountain to Tuitt's Village to see his mother and to tend his billy goat, which he had tethered next to her shack. It wouldn't do, he said, to have billy anywhere around his females—not until he was needed to make goat babies.

The day after William planted the bananas, we were astounded to see that each shoot, which he had lopped at the top with his cutlass as a parting gesture, had grown an inch, or so it seemed. At least, the core had pushed up. Bananas grow from the inside, and new leaves growing upward look like furled umbrellas. Once a leaf pushes out of the core it unwinds and opens.

To start with, a freshly unfurled banana leaf isn't shredded; fringing happens in the wind. Planted away from the wind, bananas may have intact leaves. You can come to a tropical place, though, and tell by the state of the banana leaves whether there has been a recent storm.

Pruning and chopping were a constant occupation, and the goats, many of which belonged to our friend William, were happy because Ed shared the clippings. In fact, they had become instrumentally trained so that whenever he left our gate on foot, they came running. I called Ed the "candyman."

Every now and then William would appear at our gate with goat meat meant as a gift. The first time this happened he said he had made his kill that morning. I asked, "Oh, which one?" He said it was the little male I'd seen running around with his twin, a female I had named "Nice Girl."

I said, "Oh, poor thing." I felt kind of sad.

William shrugged. "He should know that's what he was born for." Females were jealously guarded because they could produce more young. But the life of a male wasn't worth much.

I thanked him for the one plastic bag containing the goat roast and another containing a big piece of cake that Mamie had baked. We ate the cake right away, but we put the goat in the freezer. In two weeks, when I got up the nerve to thaw it out and cook it, we could pretend it had come from the grocery store. We came to call this ploy "running it through the freezer."

Our mango tree was a sad specimen, having been knocked nearly over by Hurricane Hugo. It was leaning into the yard, putting out new leaves, but nary a blossom. Meanwhile, the neighbor's mango tree, which was never watered or sprayed and which was loaded with termite trails, bore fruit and not just during the mango seasons, June and December, but more or less all year. Fortunately for us, no one was living in the house and the tree grew quite close to the fence separating our two properties. So we had ourselves a mango whenever one within easy reach was ripe.

We had been told that a Peter Smythe, one of the island's horticultural specialists, was a whiz at grafting mango trees, so we stopped off at the Grove agricultural station to see if he would come to our house to have a look. He was on vacation, but a woman in the office phoned him and let Ed make arrangements with him directly. Yes, yes, he'd be happy to come one of these days, but he didn't say when.

My broccoli was in trouble; its leaves looked like lace. I spent nearly an hour one day picking off little green worms, one by one, and squashing them. I was afraid to use very much insecticide, as I feared the plants would be burned up by the chemicals in combination with the hot sun. Katy had told me she picked the worms off, and I considered her to be the most successful farmer around.

She also said she made her own bug and worm spray —1 tablespoon dishwashing liquid and 4 tablespoons of salad oil in a bucket of water. "You can put this on Jack Spaniards ("paper wasps," as they are known in the United States), Katy said, "and it will kill them." I made her elixir, which I put into a spray bottle, and tested it on worms I found on a hibiscus bush. The worms rolled up and dropped off almost immediately.

In a couple of weeks, Peter Smythe appeared one afternoon in an ancient and rusting Land Rover owned by the government's agricultural department and announced that he had come to graft our mango tree. Smythe was a slight, white-haired man with piercing eyes and an intense manner, and I took a liking to him right away. Carrying all his tools in a plastic bag, Smythe, who was theoretically retired but who still advised the government about plant-related topics, strode into our back yard to survey our poor tree. Mainly on this day, he wanted to see if we had pruned away some of the branches as he had instructed us to do on the phone, and he wanted to determine what kinds of grafts he should bring the next day.

As for the grapefruit tree, which was also terribly beaten up by Hugo, Smythe said we should cut back dead and dying branches at a 45-degree angle so rain would run off and then paint the cuts with spray paint. After that, he said, we should break up the soil under the tree—all the way out to the drip line—with a mattock so the roots could breathe. Smythe said we should spread about five pounds of fertilizer where we had used the mattock and water it in.

When he saw that some of the grapefruit tree's branches had been hacked on with a machete, the old arborist clicked his teeth in disapproval. The machete was used by many on the island to tidy up and prune back with little regard for how the chopping affected the tree's ability to withstand insect infestation and disease.

Although he received some of his training from the University of Vermont and had worked for the Montserrat government for years, Smythe planted "by the signs." That's why he was going to come back the next day and not only graft the mango but also plant an avocado for us. The full moon was coming the following week.

True to his word, he arrived with the avocado the next day and one graft for our mango tree. He decided the best place to put the avocado would be near the bananas and asked Ed to dig a hole. Then he wanted to know which of us had the latest birthday in the year. I said I did. Smythe directed me to be the one to put the two-foot-tall tree into the hole and cover its roots with dirt.

"You should name the plant 'Carol,' and then it's sure to grow," he said," adding, "Don't tell anybody."

Smythe was often the bearer of gifts. He appeared one day, ostensibly to check on "his" plants, but he took a strange, elongated pawpaw, two cucumbers and a "shaddock" from his trunk and gave them to us, waving away my attempt to pay. All the produce came from his yard, he said, and he wanted to share it. ("Shaddock," or "pomelo," is a citrus fruit related to the grapefruit, but is much bigger, perhaps as big as a soccer ball.)

I complained about all the bugs in our garden, which were making me think of giving up horticulture. This was especially true of the broccoli. I should use insecticide often, he said, as often as every 10 days "as a preventive measure, just like contraception."

We always invited Smythe to sit on our porch and have a cold drink. It was inspiring to listen to his advice. Everywhere on the island farmers were having trouble of one kind and another, he said. One man's crop was eaten by rats. Another's, by iguanas. And still another's, by fungus. I said, "There's so much competition. It's difficult to raise anything here."

"Yes," he said, "it is difficult. But we have to try. We have to try."

He talked about his son, who had died of acute diabetes over in Antigua and about his wife, who also died. So many people revered her, he said, that at the funeral "people were crying that I didn't know knew her." After five years of loneliness, he married again.

As had become his custom, Smythe brought me a hand of bananas, this time to add to the bananas I bought earlier in the day from Katy. When Ed came home from delivering Meals on Wheels, he brought me more bananas—given to him by Lucy from a plant in her yard. They were tops among the delicious fruits we enjoyed.

PRESERVES AND PUDDING

Our guava trees were producing so many fruits that I was throwing them away. This seemed too wasteful, so I went through my cookbooks to find a good recipe that would use up a lot. I had made jelly before, but how many jars of that could two people eat? I could, however, give some for gifts.

I found a recipe for guava "fool" in the *Montserrat Cookbook*. According to the British English dictionary Tolbert had left in the living room bookcase, "fool" is a pudding made with milk, fruit and sugar, so a "fool" could, presumably, be made from peaches or apples as well as guavas.

GUAVA FOOL

Boil halved guavas until they are soft. (I used about eight the size of golf balls.)

Drain. Then run through a sieve to get rid of skins and the round, hard seeds. (This was the hardest part of preparation, and it was very hard on sieves.)

Mix in 1 tablespoon fresh-squeezed lime juice and 1 cup of sugar. Add just enough evaporated milk, stirring constantly, so that the mixture thickens, maybe half a cup. Pour into custard cups. Refrigerate until the fool reaches a pudding consistency.

We became really attached to papayas, or paw-paws as they were called, so we planted several that Nancy had started in her compost bin. We'd had no luck starting them ourselves, although they sprouted up unbidden over the summer while we were away and became large trees by the time we returned to Montserrat in December.

William had a paw-paw tree that was taller than his house, and it bore pear-shaped fruits that were often bigger than my head. I'm not aware he ever fertilized it. The plant showed up after Hurricane Huge and in a few months was huge, William said. Meanwhile, we struggled, trying some new plants every year.

One thing Nancy could not do was guarantee the sex of her plants. If they were males, they didn't produce fruits. Some said that by performing radical surgery on a male plant—cutting the stalk in a V-shape, for example—you could change the sex. I'd only read about this, but never tried it.

So, you could water and fertilize a plant, lavishing undying love and care on it, and it would reward you at maturity by showing by its flowers that it was a male. The only thing to do then was cut it down.

Billy, who worked for Nancy and her husband, stopped by while I was working in the yard. I found out more than I wanted to know about him and his family and about the families for whom he worked. He said he was supposed to go to Antigua the week before to get a tooth pulled, but he didn't go. When I quizzed him as to the reason, he said he'd go next week.

At 28 years old, he was missing several teeth, two of them in front. He said he had false teeth, but rarely wore them. I asked him if they were at home in a drawer. He said, "No."

I said, "Well, where are they?"

"In WAH-ter," he said. When Billy left, I moved around to the back yard to weed in my vegetable garden. Right away, I noticed two iguanas sitting motionless in a nearby tree. They seemed to be look-ing at me. It was a perfect spot from which to check on my vegetables and fruits and to make decisions about what seemed ripe for harvest. I tried to dislodge the beasts with a rock and, then, with the garden hose. They didn't move. Later, when Ed was cutting the grass, he nearly ran over one of them—or its cousin. He hurried into the house for the camera, and I enticed the iguana, about three feet long, to eat hibiscus blossoms I tossed onto the ground in front of him.

Had we been fleeter of foot and less disgusted by the thought, we might have had iguana stew for dinner. I found a recipe in the *Montserrat Cookbook*. (See the recipes at the end of this book.)

Billy was always full of village news, and I was the lucky recipient. "You know the donkey that's been tied back there [behind our house] for two days?" Of course we knew; the poor animal, which had no water and nothing to eat but dry grass, had been braying loudly in complaint.

"Yes, we know," I said.

He belongs to a man up in the village, Billy said, who is beside himself because "he lost his woman." Billy admitted the woman fi-nally left because the man beat her once too many times. Ed told Billy he had never beaten me and that beating up on another hu-man being was always wrong, no matter what the circumstances. The woman should have left after he beat her the first time, Ed said. Billy didn't quite know if he believed that was true. In any case, losing your woman was no excuse for treating your animals cruelly, we told him. "Maybe what we need to do is find the man another woman," Ed joked.

The Stewarts had known Billy since he was a small boy. He was teased unmercifully because of his stutter, and the children up in Tuitt's, his village, stole things from him, the memory of which had carried over into his adult life, Nancy Stewart said.

The week before, he had brought her a pair of pants on which to sew a button. When she was done with that minor repair, she also pressed the pants. Before he took them home, he asked Nancy to put the pants in a bag. She said he always wanted everything given to him to be put into a bag—perhaps so no one would know what he was carrying. Maybe he feared that whatever he had would be taken away. She told him the pants would become wrinkled, but he insisted.

There was a fungus, or mold or leaf-eating insects on one plant or the other all the time, or so it seemed. While we were in town one day, I carried with me a branch of hibiscus with a curious growth among the leaves and took it to the Grove for assessment. The expert there said my hibiscus was suffering from the mite that had been plaguing the island for two and a half years. He wasn't sure I'd be able to eradicate it. I could cut off the infected parts, he said, and burn them, then spray what was left with Sevin. Or, I could do nothing.

Although I thought he was kidding, I soon figured he was serious when he told me to take my branch back to "the East" and not put it down anywhere in Plymouth. They didn't want that stuff over in the West to infect hibiscus there.

I asked for Sevin in the room where pesticides and herbicides were sold at the Grove, and Brian Cassell asked if I wanted one pound or ten. I inquired how strong the solution for spraying the hibiscus needed to be, and he said I should use a matchbox full of Sevin per gallon of water. (In an experiment at home later, I discovered that a matchbox was 1 1/3 tablespoons.)

The cashew tree in our backyard flourished when other plants died. The nuts were surprising in that each one grew at the bottom of an apple-like fruit. The apple, called a "cherry" by Montserratians, had a slightly tart taste and was quite juicy. I gave Katy some and

William some and still never ran out. William told us that the nuts had extremely toxic husks, which had to be burned off. He said he would collect the nuts until there were enough to "process," and then he would show us what to do.

Collecting enough nuts took several months, but one day William said he had enough and invited us to come over to his house. Ed and I sat in the shade while he built a fire of twigs, coconut husks and an old piece of cast-off lumber. When the fire was blazing well, he placed the lid from an oil drum on the fire. A woman friend there to witness the spectacle said she would have bored holes in the lid to let the toxic oil from the cashews drain off.

William paid no attention, but arranged the cashew "seeds" on the lid and stirred them with a stick, trying to get them evenly hot. At last, the oil began to burn. The fire was fiercely hot, and the presence of the oil was like throwing gasoline onto a burning trash heap. The smoke was black, copious and acrid. As the wind shifted, we had to move our chairs.

When the fire had burned down somewhat, William poured the seeds off onto the ground. In just a couple of minutes, not long enough for them to cool, in my opinion, he began handling them with his bare hands and gave some to his friend and some to Ed and me. He then instructed us to find a flat stone to place the nuts on and another with which to pound them. The goal was to break off the blackened outer skin.

This was a dirty, oily job, even though the husks came off easily. After pounding and picking for some time, we were able to assemble only enough finished cashews to fill three soup cans. I understood then why cashew nuts are so expensive.

The cashew tree with its strange fruits and nuts could have been used as a prop for a horror movie. One night about 9 p.m., Ed heard whooshing noises in our backyard; they seemed to be coming from one of the trees, but it was too dark to tell which one. I had heard similar weird noises the night before about midnight and thought we might have a prowler, but didn't go to check because both Ed and Wishard were asleep.

A powerful flashlight showed that the sounds were being made by perhaps as many as thirty large fruit bats, which were feasting on the cashew "cherries," hanging on them to get a bite and flapping their wings as they shifted positions in the tree. I would judge that these bats had at least a 12-inch wingspan, maybe more.

9

ISLAND WAYS

Despite off and on rain, we drove to Harris' up the mountain from Spanish Point to attend a street festival put on by the Harris' Methodist Church. That building was totally destroyed in Hurricane Hugo, but was rebuilt by parishioners with the help of teams from the United States.

The street festival, the proceeds of which went to the rebuilding effort, was held across the street from the church in the ruins of a waiting station for bus passengers, also damaged by the hurricane. We'd been told that the festival was a good place to buy "goat water." We had no idea what that was, but our initial reaction was we certainly didn't want to eat—or drink—any of THAT!

But Sharon, who was already at work helping with the open-air cooking, encouraged us to try what was an island specialty. In fact, she said, good goat water makers were known island-wide. So we agreed to try a cup.

The Harris' version was simmered over open fires in five-gallon lard cans, as women in bright, flowered skirts tended them, and calypso music boomed from loudspeakers. Some of the women, members of the little Methodist congregation, also were frying chicken in iron skillets.

Little tables held cakes, soft drinks and another local dish we were encouraged to try called "duckana." That may not be the correct spelling, but the Montserratian women I talked to weren't sure how the word was spelled. This dish is pureed sweet potato, coconut, brown sugar, allspice, nutmeg and almond extract—all mixed together, then, as they made it, rolled up and tied in a piece of banana leaf and steamed.

Goat Water Isn't What You Think: It's Good

Actually, goat water is not watery at all, but is made of goat meat in a kind of stew, simmered for hours with cloves, onions, garlic, thyme, marjoram, mace, rum and hot peppers. The gravy which results is darkened with what was known locally as "browning," a concoction made by Crosse and Blackwell.

Goat rib bones stick out of the top when the stew is served from a Styrofoam cup.

I joked later that the recipe for this island delicacy is simple: Peel one goat and chop coarsely before simmering in water with a lot of herbs and spices and some booze.

Goat Water
(This recipe could be cut in half for a small family.)
2 quarters goat or sheep - or even some beef
4 onions, cut up
thyme, maybe a teaspoon
3/4 cup cooking oil
3 ounces fresh marjoram
4 cloves of garlic, minced
1 tablespoon whole cloves, crushed
1 tablespoon mace
2 tablespoons catsup
1 hot green pepper, whole (optional)
salt and pepper to taste

Cut the meat into 2-inch cubes, being sure to leave bones in. Wash in salt water and place in a large saucepan. Cover with cold water, bring to a boil, and simmer, covered, for 5 minutes. Skim, and continue simmering, covered, adding remaining ingredients; add boiling water as necessary. When meat is nearly tender, combine 2 cups flour with enough cold water to make a smooth paste. Stir enough of this mixture into the stew to give desired thickness, and add some browning (Kitchen Bouquet or Crosse and Blackwell) for color. Half cover the pot and continue simmering until meat is done. Add some whisky or rum if desired. Serve in cups or bowls, very hot, with the bones.

Adapted from the *Montserrat Cookbook*.

Duckana, a real sweet treat, could be baked in an oven-proof dish, without the banana leaf, and called "sweet potato pudding." (See the recipes at the end of this book.) Ever thereafter, Montserratian women giggled when I told them I liked duckana. Apparently, not many tourists knew what it was, much less had ever tasted it.

A custom adapted by expatriates for life on Montserrat was "fourzies." This was the cocktail hour, which was held starting at 4 p.m. It wasn't that people wanted to start drinking early; it was the fact that sunset near the equator year around was between 6 and 6:30 p.m. By having the cocktail hour at 4, guests could be safely home by the time the sun went down.

Even in our small neighborhood, cocktail guests drove their cars to fourzies instead of walking. Maybe the guests, retirees all, feared falling on the uneven roads. Maybe they were afraid of stepping in cow pies in the dark, or running into a cow on the loose, both real worries. Maybe they didn't want to walk uphill, which was necessary no matter where you went on the island, either going or coming. There was usually a line of cars parked in the grass outside the gate of the house where we went for fourzies.

But these events had become infrequent by the time we arrived on the scene. Helen told us that the neighborhood had changed. There was not nearly as much visiting back and forth, and there had been a drastic reduction in the celebration of fourzies. Personally, I thought the decline in drinking was a good thing.

We were told that when Spanish Point was founded in the 1970s, there was a lot of partying. Many of the older settlers, however, had died. Some of the houses were now empty, owned by Montserratians living in England or Canada who weren't yet retired. A few were owned by non-resident Canadians, who showed up for a month or so each winter.

Without fourzies, there wasn't much entertainment on the Eastside of the island except occasional dinners at neighbors' homes or fund-raisers at churches or the school. But we were content. We did receive invitations to a cocktail party at the newly restored Governor's Mansion, an event to raise money for the Montserrat National Trust. The governor, who was British, showed us around, noting that all the furniture had to be thrown out during the restoration because it was infested with termites. It seemed, he said, that the British government maintained for years it didn't have the funds for the upkeep of the home and that Montserrat should foot the expenses.

Predictably, Montserrat said it didn't have the money and that Britain should pay. As a result, nobody paid, and the house was falling into ruin. The British government said it wanted to bulldoze the building and start over, but preservationists prevailed. I noticed a photograph of Queen Elizabeth and Prince Philip of England on an end table—sort of like a picture of the Pope in the offices of a Roman Catholic archbishop.

That cocktail party was, well, a cocktail party. During some repartee, an acquaintance from the Westside of the island told us how her husband had recently broken his leg falling in the yard. Ed got into it with one of our Spanish Point neighbors, a British woman with a tart tongue. He told her she looked well, much better than before. The more he said the more he put his foot into it. She wanted to know before when. He said "before last spring." She said that, actually, she felt worse. Then another woman told this neighbor her hair looked nice. It seemed shorter and was quite becoming, the woman said. Our neighbor said that, actually, she was letting it grow.

Although taking our pets to the island had been quite a hassle, our dog Wishard paid for his expenses one night not long after the cocktail party. We were watching cricket highlights on Antigua TV—a game we were still trying to figure out—when Wishard ran to our bedroom barking and growling. Then he ran to the front door where he sniffed the air and growled again.

This was highly suspicious coming from a dog that spent most of his time sleeping, so Ed went out on the porch to investigate. I heard him yell, "What the hell are you doing in my yard? Get out." A young man, possibly just a child, stood just inside our gate, which was already locked for the night. Unable to escape easily, he immediately turned and ran toward the other end of our property and disappeared over the fence.

Just outside our bedroom window was the flat roof of the garage. We concluded that the young man was probably peering into the bedroom from this roof, hoping to see a wallet or purse within reach on top of a chest of drawers. And then Wishard foiled his plans. Other robberies had occurred on the island just that way, silently, through a slit screen. The next day, when we told Vic Henry about it, he said Ed had done exactly the right thing by yelling. The would-be burglar will never be back, Henry said, because he knows you are alert and have a big dog.

There were societal rules regarding such thievery. Burglars did not vandalize except for gaining access through slits in the screens. No windows were to be broken. Thievery was carried out through stealth, and a major goal was to stay away from victims. Conversely, victims did not physically confront thieves. By following these unwritten rules, no one got hurt.

As far as I know, the only people on Montserrat who had access to guns, in addition to the police, were men who had permission to shoot feral pigs in the island's landfill. Gradually, I'm afraid this tight gun control loosened. While we were up north one summer, we heard about a gasoline service station that was held up by someone carrying a pistol.

Up north or "bock-up" as Montserratians called that place where snowbirds went to their other life that was not on the island, we carried on as we always had, seeing Indianapolis friends and our grown children, taking occasional trips, going for doctor and dentist appointments and shopping. I had retired, but Ed was still working, although he complained about having "to put out fires"—correct snafus, sometimes caused by the insurance companies. Yet, it was still fun to have long-time clients where he could meet them face to face. After all, he had been in the business by that time about 35 years.

Where people lived on Montserrat, officially at least, was unknown to most people, whether Montserratian or expat. There were no street signs and no building numbers, for example, in downtown Plymouth, except for one, at the junction of Church Road going north, Evergreen going south and Marine Drive heading west. This practice of anonymity was dangerous to health and safety, especially should a fire break out, the fire chief said.

As new roads were built on the island, as people moved and businesses relocated, the fire department was at an increasing disadvantage. No longer did everyone know where Lawyer Piper or Nurse Evans lived. The fire department couldn't respond to an emergency run based on an urgent message to "come to the second house on the roundabout past Fred Smith's garage."

It was particularly difficult for the uninitiated to find their way around, e.g., people who didn't know where Mr. Brades' store was. You almost had to know the island, even to have been born there, to find out who and what were where.

Some of the towns on the island had no identifying signs. None of the streets, except the ones mentioned, was marked, although they all had names. Buildings, even downtown on main streets, had no numbers. Since no mail was delivered to individual houses and places of business, a numbering system didn't seem to be a high priority until the fire department spoke up about the problem.

Expatriates and Montserratians put on a musical program to raise money for signage.

When we drove into town, we were always on the lookout for people that needed rides. We learned a lot about the island that way, particularly if our passengers were talkative—and most were. Car ownership on the island was only for the more well-to-do, and many people didn't know how to drive. There were taxis, but they charged about $1 US for a ride into Plymouth, where the grocery and hardware stores were. The condition of the roads was no doubt a deterrent for them as it was for me.

Since so many people were willing to pick up hitchhikers, there was no reason to worry about transportation. Two of our frequent passengers were Mamie and William, our neighbors down the hill. On one occasion, while William was tending his animals, we took Mamie into town to pick up food for his 90-year-old mother. She lived in a tiny house up in Tuitt's Village, a settlement up the mountain from Spanish Point. Earlier, William had told us that he was "the only child my mother ever had," yet he was quick to add that he had several brothers and sisters. It took us a while to figure out what this all meant.

A waitress in one of the restaurants in downtown Plymouth told us, in response to a general question about her family, "My mother had no sons, and my father had no sons." Yet she had brothers. Hmmm.

These odd and inexplicable truths were taken matter-of-factly on Montserrat. They were part of reality and nothing to worry over, contemplate or, even, think about. Mamie and William's mother did not get along, so there was no thought that the old woman would be moving in with the couple. Mamie said that William's mother didn't think he was being well taken care of.

There was a confusion about William's last name. I knew him as William Owensby, but many of the villagers called him William Brown. That's because his father was a Mr. Brown, but William sometimes went by the last name of his mother, which was Owensby. He was listed in the phone book as William Owensby. Other Montserratians had similar dual names; it was difficult for outsiders to figure out who was who.

"When you aren't a legal child, you can't go by your father's name," William said. When he registered for school in Bethel as a little boy many years before, he was known as William Brown, but when he went to England to work, legally, he was William Owensby. He said many people up in the village would not know who I was talking about, however, if I called him "William Owensby."

William appeared at our gate one morning to ask if we were going to town. He was carrying a large, stiff fish wrapped in a garbage bag. A "chap" had caught the fish, William said. And not too recently, judging from the smell and from the rigor mortis. William said he personally didn't have the money to buy the fish, so he was taking it to a supermarket to sell.

Carlton, a young man from Tuitt's Village who lived in the ruin of a house down the hill from us near the sea, was a frequent passenger. He had been given a Hugo House by the government, but he preferred not to live there, nor with his mother. He had some sort of disability, but we were never sure just what it was. Actually, he was being cared for by all the villagers, and by those who lived in Spanish Point.

Trying to keep a conversation going with Carlton was sometimes difficult, but I thought of a not-so-facile conversation starter. In fact, it sounds quite silly now that I'm writing it. "Do you have a cow?" I asked, figuring that Montserratians liked to talk about their animals.

"I had one," Carlton said, "but she went blank." We couldn't figure out what that meant, but I finally came to the conclusion that what he was trying to tell us was that the cow ceased having calves. Going blank would be reason enough to sell a cow.

Several days later, Carlton brought along a pal, a man we had seen before but whose name we didn't know. He always wore a cowboy hat. When Ed asked his name, the man said, "I'm Jesse James."

"That's not such a good name," I teased. "Jesse James was a bad guy."

Carlton suggested that maybe the guy should call himself "Sammy Davis Jr."

We asked Jesse James if he could dance a la Sammy Davis Jr. "Yes I can," he said. "I took lessons in England."

We learned later that Jesse James was squatting in a boarded-up shack in one of the villages and sometimes took showers in the community shower building. In fact, he asked to be let out of our car across the road from Katy Connor's house. That was the location of the neighborhood shower.

Another Spanish Point neighbor was Evelyn Sweeney, whose parents had a private outdoor shower. They lived in a tiny wood house across the street from the concrete block home Evelyn had just built for her retirement. A nurse/midwife on St. Thomas for 20 years, she had moved back to Montserrat to care for her aged parents.

She had given her father a shower that morning, his first in several days "because the water has been too cold," she said when we were having tea one day. She explained the temperature of the water by alluding to the fact that it had been cloudy lately. Water for the shower came from a garden hose, which was heated by the sun.

Montserratians who didn't have running water inside their houses or a hose hook-up as her father did used the village's "pipe" and carried water home, heated it in the sun or on the stove and poured it over themselves. Or they could use the community shower, as Jesse James did.

Outdoor showers at private homes were not obvious until you looked closely and put two and two together. Usually, they were enclosures four to six feet on a side made of old galvanized roofing with either a shower head or a jerry-rigged garden hose. At first, I thought such enclosures were outhouses. Some people also had those. One day, I had an "aha moment" when I saw an enclosure with a bath towel slung over one of the walls.

In any case, you would have to get used to showering in tepid water: not a problem when it was at least 75 degrees outside. But the supply of sun-warmed water was finite, and your shower might turn cold if you didn't move fast enough.

Before I left, Evelyn showed me her garden, in which she was growing a bit of everything for her table. She said she had been wanting a small coconut palm that would never grow tall so she could reach the fruits more easily. Although she didn't know if it was true, she had been told that if the gardener sat down while planting a coconut palm, it would stay small. I told her I was skeptical.

When our wastebaskets were full, we loaded bags of trash into the car and drove them up the hill, across the street from the health clinic, to the community dump. In three winters on the island, garbage pick-up hadn't improved. By the time the truck came to clean out the 15 x 6 waste enclosure, garbage and trash spilled over the top.

I hated going to the dump because of the smell and because rats scurried out when we threw our bags in. Every village had at least one of these dumps, and it was quite obvious to me why the island had a rat problem. Now and then, island officials would encourage residents to clean up around their homes and put out traps and poison in an effort to eradicate the rats, but no one seemed to figure out that as long as there were village dumps, eradication was impossible.

It was quite ironic, I thought, that the Bethel dump was across the narrow street and down the hill a bit from the walk-in clinic, where nurses sat on the porch and waited for customers.

Margaret Joseph, the president of the Bethel Methodist Church congregation, once told me the island recipe for rat poison, in case we ever needed to use some at home:

Two cups of corn meal

1/4 cup brake fluid

Some years trash collection was better than others. That probably had something to do with the road worthiness of the garbage trucks or whether the garbage workers were on the job. At times, the dump enclosure remained unemptied for several weeks. What was ironic about the situation was the fact that the Public Works Department (PWD) trucks had to drive by the garbage pit on their way to the island's landfill.

Ed generated the following poster on our computer: "PWD Please clean out our house. It's getting crowded in here. Signed: De Rats." While he was taping the poster to the concrete block sides of the trash collection bin, two rats ran back and forth inside. We wondered if PWD would do anything.

One afternoon, Ed carried a shovel and some gloves up the hill to make the dump area more presentable. When it reached "almost full," some people began placing their trash bags on the ground near, but not in, the enclosure. Needless to say, roaming dogs, feral pigs and rats had a wonderful time.

Our next to last year on the island, we learned that Dr. Tommy Wagner, one of the island's family practice physicians, had become so alarmed about the potential spread of disease at the village dumps that he formed a company, Opal Enterprises, to take over garbage and trash collection from the government. The take-over would not occur for several months, however; I suspected the government-paid trash haulers would stop making pick-ups, particularly in the East. Many of the expats who lived in the West already had private trash haulers and paid by the month for the service. Most of them wouldn't stand for the conditions we endured on the Eastside of the island.

Infrastructure work was agonizingly slow. The three-mile stretch of road from Plymouth to the town of Cork Hill on the Westside was under reconstruction for months, with many lane closures and traffic back-ups. When driving toward the co-op where we bought chlorine "pucks" for our swimming pool, we noticed a new, hand-painted sign beside the road. It read "Slow Road Work." We laughed out loud.

Although we were aware it was not possible to work fast or for long hours in the heat, the speed with which this construction was being completed was ridiculous. The expansion/widening was started in June, and it was nowhere nearly complete six months later when we returned to the island for the winter season. When finished, the road was supposed to have a wide path at the side so people could walk into Plymouth, and the two driving lanes were to be widened as well. It would be straight and over flat terrain. Some people were worried that the road would become a racetrack, which, in fact, happened with disastrous results about a year later.

We were unhappy about changes being made more speedily along Marine Drive, which, before construction, gave an unobstructed view of the ocean. It was promised that the small shanty bars built for carnival season would be torn down immediately afterward, but we were skeptical about the speed at which this would occur. If they had been spread out a bit, we could have seen the Caribbean from along the shore downtown, but the bars were built less than 10 feet apart.

10
SIMPLE PLEASURES

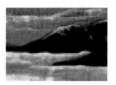

Because we lived only about two miles up the hill from the airport, and our view was unobstructed, we rapidly became experts on the comings and goings of the planes. Planes are supposed to face into the prevailing wind when they land. Since the prevailing winds in our area were nearly always from the South, the planes had to head toward the cliff before turning and setting down on the runway. When the prevailing winds were from the north, however, planes had to land from the south.

That meant excitement for us as the small aircraft passed by our house at eye level, down the mountain slope about 800 yards. We could tell what was going to happen by the noise of the approaching plane, and we dropped everything to run outside and watch the spectacle from our porch—with binoculars, of course.

We also became aware when planes were not on schedule. "Hey, Ed, the 9 o'clock is just coming in, and it's 10:15," I would say. We sometimes ran outside to see if the incoming plane was the scheduled airline LIAT (Leeward Island Air Transport, or, as we sometimes called it, "Leave Island Any Time.") Or the plane could be a charter, which could show up at any time. We were never starved for something to do.

The 7:30 p.m. flight from Antigua was the last of the day. We could tell if the plane was on its way when the landing lights came on at the Montserrat airport. That's because, to save money, the Montserrat authorities never flipped the switch until notified that a plane had taken off from Antigua 27 miles away.

When guests from the States were staying with us, one of the entertainments a day or so after their arrival was to drive a bit up what we called "The North Road" and park a few minutes before a plane was due to land. Seeing the plane seemingly head straight for the cliff just below where we were sitting before turning abruptly and setting down on the runway always was shocking to our guests. And it never ceased being a thrill for us.

Sometimes, when we had no guests, Ed and I would drive down to the airport, buy a bag of M&M's, our favorite snack, drive up to our favorite spot along "The North Road" and eat our candy while waiting for the plane.

Even on holidays, if there wasn't a neighborhood get-together, we would do whatever work we needed to do, have our swim and drive to the airport for M&M's. On one Christmas afternoon, we took our candy and drove to Trant's Bay beach just to the north of the runway to watch for the arrival of the 4:45 p.m. LIAT plane. It would, once it turned to avoid the cliff, pass by nearly over our heads. We got our thrills the best—and safest—way we could.

In talking about this particular piece of land I should say that we saw a family was cooking over an open fire on the beach, but not one of them was putting so much as a toe in the water. Full of boulders, undertow and huge waves, Trant's Bay was not a good place to swim. Our friend Evelyn Sweeney pronounced the beach down by the airport as "ha-ZARD-us."

Our activities changed with the seasons. For example, as the afternoon waned on a typical day in spring, we sat on the porch and watched a pair of flycatchers tending their nest on top of a transformer on an electric light pole a few feet from our fence. There were no chicks yet, but the parents were protective of the nest nonetheless and noisily chased away any dove or cattle egret that flew too near.

Every now and then, the flycatchers swooped down to our swimming pool to get a drink and dampen their feathers. We found their antics endlessly interesting. To us, then, in that place, this activity, or lack thereof, seemed in no way a waste of time. To just sit and "be" was initially a little difficult for "Type A" people such as ourselves. To tell the truth, however, we had practiced for these Montserrat moments without knowing it years before when tent camping with our children. One day back then, for example, we sat for an hour or more and watched a spider spin a web.

Taking walks after dark was a peaceful way to spend part of an evening. When the moon was full, we did this without a flashlight, staying mostly on the roads near our house. You did have to be careful of fresh cow manure, but only the fresh "meadow muffins" were a problem. They dried out in half a day in the sun.

Actually, finding the whole cow in one's path was more of a problem than stepping in its poop. Bossy lying in the road chewing her cud could easily be seen on a moonlit night. Getting her to move out of the way was something else again. Contented cows are, well, contented to stay where they are.

We drove around a lot to become acquainted with the various villages on the island. One day, our adventure took us to Long Ground, which was up the mountain and south of us. To get there, Ed drove through the tiny Tuitt's Village and then headed along a narrow, twisty road with drop-offs, sometimes on both sides, up, up and up for a mile or so, until we came to the even tinier town. The paved road ended just beyond the Pentecostal Church where William and Mamie worshipped. I was amazed that they sometimes walked to church from Spanish Point.

Some of the best farmland on the island was still farther up the mountain above Long Ground. The soil was richer, and rainfalls were greater than in Spanish Point, which was only two and a half miles away down the mountain as the crow flew.

The view of the sea from Long Ground was spectacular, but it was easy to see why the hurricane had been so destructive up there. The town took the full brunt of the wind, with wooden shacks clinging to cliffs as high as 2,000 feet above sea level. Many houses still showed signs of damage, and pieces of galvanized roofing littered the ground. Several cars, their windows broken and vines growing in and out, sat derelict beside the road.

I noticed what I was convinced was marijuana growing in a patch beside the road. It didn't look as if it had just sprung up there, as it grew in rows, albeit irregular rows. We subsequently learned that relatively inaccessible towns such as Molyneaux, which was close to Plymouth, and Long Ground were notorious for being the island's centers for illicit pot, known locally as "weed." Some also was grown back in the bush in areas accessible only by donkey.

We later learned that this plant we saw was probably not marijuana at all, but cassava, a root vegetable which is used as a starch in the diet and in powder form is tapioca. If it's not prepared correctly, however, cassava (or manioc as it's sometimes called) can be poisonous.

Until we bought a washing machine, we drove into Plymouth to use the coin laundry. This, too, became a chance for simple pleasures; we bought pastries and locally made soda while our clothes were washing and sat on a nearby concrete wall to have our snack. A hen and her two chicks might scratch around in the dust nearby, and in a nearby field a cow might be chomping on grass. Just beyond was the turquoise sea.

Driving home to the Eastside, we rounded a bend and descended into Harris', where we could see from high up the little Anglican church perched on the mountainside. We remarked to each other that it was hard to believe we lived in such a beautiful place.

Occasionally, we went out to dinner in one of the few restaurants open at night. A particular favorite was the Blue Dolphin, up a twisty mountain road in the southern part of Montserrat. When we arrived, the restaurant, really the porch of a private home, was almost always empty. We concluded that Montserratians, as a rule, did not eat away from home for pocketbook reasons, and white expats were afraid to drive at night on the narrow, winding roads with drop-offs and loose animals.

We liked the Blue Dolphin because it faced west, and from our table we could watch as the sun dropped into the sea. Not to mention that it was fun to watch the lizards climbing the walls in search of insects that were attracted to the lights. When you called to make a reservation at the Blue Dolphin, the person answering the phone wanted to know what you would like to eat. I came to believe that the cook would go out the day of your dinner and buy just enough food to feed you and only you. Although our choice of meat might vary, we always asked for candied plantains and sweet potatoes in some form.

In order to raise money for the town of Lee's, a man who worked for the Grove and a woman from the electric company led a hike through the mysterious bamboo forest, a tourist attraction on the island, and we signed up to go. To get to the forest, we had to walk down into what was known as Galway's Soufriere before climbing up the other side of the basin.

What Does Soufriere Mean?

According to Dr. Howard A. Fergus, Montserrat's historian, the term "soufriere" might be of French Creole origin and in the West Indies means any volcanic activity reaching the surface of the earth, including fumaroles and hot springs as well as volcanoes themselves. These features are present on many Caribbean islands. For example, a volcano on Guadeloupe is called "Grande Soufriere."

Wikipedia on the Internet defines the word "soufriere" as "sulfur outlet." Many Montserratians dug sulfur as a means of making money. Although we didn't know it, there were eight such sulfur outlets on the island when we lived there. The main one, however, was Galway's Soufriere. Somewhere underneath the steaming sulfur outlets was a volcano.

There had been no eruption of a Montserrat volcano that anybody knew of since the 1500s or 1600s, depending on whatever source you read or to whomever you talked. And before that, oh, not for 18,000 or 19,000 years. That's what was taught in schools, according to Dr. Fergus in the 1996 book of history, poetry, essays and reports that he edited, *Eruption: Montserrat Versus Volcano*.

The bamboo forest was the habitat of the Montserrat Oriole, a bird found in the world only on our island, and going bird-watching to view it was an activity we enjoyed. Most of the 750 orioles thought to exist lived in the bamboos, but a few had been spotted in other parts of the island where tree cover was favorable.

We got up at 5 a.m. on the designated day so we could eat a quick breakfast and drive to the trailhead, where our leader met us. A group of teen-agers, a woman from the electric company and a couple of men who lived near the airport joined us. While we were sliding and walking and sliding and walking down the slippery slope to the soufriere vents, our leader told us this end of the island—the south—was only 200,000 years old, and he added that the vigorous steaming and belching of boiling hot mud was what kept the volcano from erupting more energetically. So he said.

As soon as we climbed out of the sulfur pit, the leaves on philodendron plants appeared huge, and we soon saw the yellow blossoms of the heliconia plant, which is a relative of the banana. The cup-shaped petals of the heliconia, arranged like stacks of tiny yellow canoes on the central stalk, were quite hard and held water, which was drunk by the Montserrat Oriole.

Our leader from the Grove had brought a small recorder on which he intended to play a tape of the call of a male oriole, thinking, he said, that a real bird, hearing the call, might show himself to defend his territory. As we walked along, the woman from the electric company, who was well versed on the natural history of the island, showed us various plants and explained their uses.

Several she pointed out could be used for "bush tea." These had various medicinal purposes, from curing headaches to settling the stomach to easing pre-menstrual cramps. Our leader told us that guava leaves infused in boiling water would cure diarrhea.

A little farther along the trail, we came to our first bamboo. But we walked on, thinking perhaps that we would be more likely to see birds in the center of the forest— which, indeed, did turn out to be the case. There trees were as big around as saucers and 50 to 75 feet tall. Very little light reached the forest floor. Our leader put a finger to his lips, listened and pointed out to us the call of the oriole. He set up the tape recorder, and then, sure enough, came the reply of another oriole, which approached and sat high in a bamboo tree overhead. It was a black, orange and yellow bird about nine inches long, from what I could tell as it moved very fast through the semi-dark canopy.

We all got excited, as birdwatchers do, pointed and oohed and ahhed and made fools of ourselves, even though we saw the bird for only a split second before our oohing and ahhing chased it away.

Another hike was to take us from the Galway's Soufriere, the same place that was the start of our hike to see the Montserrat Oriole, to the Tar River Estate. That was the ruin of a mansion up the mountain and to the south of where we lived in Spanish Point. A couple of years later, the Tar River Estate became the center of attention because of the volcano.

To beat the heat, we arose at 5:30 a.m. and ate a quick breakfast before walking to a neighbor's house to climb into the back of his truck and be taken to the trailhead. The hikers were two Canadian tourists; two German women named Hildegard who were renting a house in Spanish Point; T.J., the tour leader; Ed and I. Kris, T.J.'s wife, rode up front. She would drive the truck back home and wait for our return.

It was chilly for Montserrat—69.5 degrees at 6:30 a.m.—so T.J. drove slowly through Plymouth and down to the soufriere. That way, he thought, we wouldn't all be cold.

As we were waiting to start the hike, two Rastafarians rode up on donkeys. In lieu of saddles, they were sitting on two-foot-square pieces of foam rubber. They told us they ride every morning up to Roche's Estate, another mansion ruin, where they farm. This was no doubt a trek, even on donkey back, and I was impressed by their tenacity.

What Is Rastafari?

When Haile Selassie I became King of Ethiopia in 1930, a new religion, called Rastafari, was born. Its adherents believe that the king, who reigned until his death in 1974, was the second coming of Jesus. At first, Rastafari adherents lived principally in Jamaica, but now they can be found all over the world.

Many of their beliefs coincide with those of the Jewish and Christian religions, but there are important differences. The principal one is the use of marijuana—or ganja—as part of spiritual practice, along with drumming, chanting and meditating. Rastas, as they prefer to be called, reject materialism and believe that Ethiopia was the birthplace of humankind.

Although Rastas usually wear their hair in dreadlocks, (naturally tangled, coiled and grown long) some people in other cultures also wear that style. Dreadlocks among Rastafari are often covered by knitted or crocheted caps of red, green, gold and sometimes black. Green, gold and red are the colors of the Ethiopian flag.

The musician Bob Marley brought the Rastafari way of life to the world's attention in the 1970s.

The path down to the soufriere was quite steep and hazardous because the rocks were soft and crumbly, and water in the streams was boiling hot. There were, of course, no guard rails. These little problems, though, were nothing compared to what was to come.

First, we climbed up to the bamboo forest, where Ed and I had walked earlier with the Lee's Action Group. We had thought that hike, to the end of the bamboo forest, was excruciatingly long in the hot sun, so I steeled myself for a much longer walk and hoped I'd be able to keep up.

According to the map, the hike was to be about 4 miles, give or take a little, and the contour lines were close together, meaning that the terrain was "hilly." In the beginning, we slogged through a lot of mud, tall weeds and over rocks, up hill and down, until we finally reached Roche's Estate, which dated from the mid-1800s. At least that was the date we surmised because some equipment rusting in the sun nearby was stamped with 18--(illegible). Apparently, it was used for growing and processing sugar cane—no doubt with slave labor.

On part of our hike, we walked along roads used by oxcarts to supply the estate. The sugar mill, a cone-shaped structure where the sugar cane was boiled, overlooked Long Ground, with Spanish Point in the distance. With binoculars, we could see this sugar mill from our backyard.

We took long drinks of water and sat down in the grass in a shady spot to rest, a good thing because the trail from Roche's to the end of our walk turned really nasty. First, we had to climb down, down, down to the edge of a ghaut and then up some very steep concrete steps, which had been put in years ago, I believe, by the Montserrat Water Authority. At one time, there was a water source, perhaps a spring, in the area.

Ed told me later it was fortuitous I didn't look down as I was climbing the steps, because there was a huge drop-off. I had enough to do to negotiate the steps, which had risers about two feet high and an iron pipe railing. It was broken in some places and sagging in others. As my knees were quivering with fatigue by this point, I made the climb by laying my walking stick down on a step and hauling myself up on my knees.

We all made the climb successfully and then began the ascent up to the Tar River Estate, up a former road, which also was quite steep. What was worse was that the road was exposed to the sun. By then, it was 1 p.m., and we had been on the trail 5 1/2 hours.

By the time we arrived at the estate house, I was not only hungry and thirsty, I was also somewhat nauseated, not a good sign. T.J.'s wife, who had become alarmed because we weren't back as soon as she thought we should be, had driven their beat-up truck over a rocky, rutted path to reach the estate house to await our arrival. The paved road ended in Long Ground. To say her presence was a welcome sight is an understatement.

Back home, a tepid shower never felt so good, and my peanut butter on homemade bread never tasted so good.

Most mornings we watched the sun come up. The sky turned a pale orange first with accents of bright yellow on the frilly edges of clouds to show where the sun would appear. Then, a tiny sliver of sun showed above the horizon, growing bigger quickly, until, in a few seconds, the fiery disk cleared the surface of the water, and you had to look away.

Sunrise on December 17 was 6:25 a.m., and the sun set that day at 5:35 p.m. The swings in the Midwest are much greater. The Indianapolis sunrise on that same day was 8 a.m., and the sunset was 5:21 p.m.

Watching the moonrise, especially at the time of the full moon, became a ritual for us. On the nights when the moon rose after dark and before bedtime, we would plop down in chairs on our porch 30 minutes to an hour before we thought the drama would take place, based on the date of the full moon in previous months. We who lived close to the land kept track of such things.

Normally, both the sea and the sky melded in inky blackness. The sign that the drama of moonrise was about to occur was subtle at first: The sky became infinitesimally lighter near the horizon, light enough that it was possible to differentiate sea and sky. As the minutes passed, the contrast intensified. If there were a few clouds, either darker or lighter than the sky, moonrise was even more spectacular.

All of a sudden, as we watched, the tip of the moon crept silently above the horizon, and immediately sent shimmers of light over the sea in a bright band. And the darkness was no more. Within a few minutes, I could read a book while standing in our backyard. The drama, the expectation of what was to come, never stopped thrilling us, no matter how many times we witnessed the spectacle.

We made arrangements to walk with Katy to an island phenomenon called the "Great Alp Falls," where we planned to shoot video to send to our granddaughter. Although Katy had lived on Montserrat all her life, she had never been to the falls.

I had teased her earlier, asking if she planned to wear shoes — as she tended not to, even on uneven terrain and when walking on rocks. I remember how once, when I asked her if she had any pawpaws for sale, she quickly took off her shoes, ran down a stony embankment and picked two ripe fruits from one of her trees. But on the hike morning, she wore sneakers, along with a flowered skirt, a striped blouse and a black hat squashed down on her braids.

As we drove south on the island through the little town of St. Patrick's, Katy announced that, given the choice of living in St. Patrick's or Long Ground, she'd prefer to live in the latter. When we asked why, she replied that Long Ground was green. For whatever reason—and some said it was because of the literally thousands of feral goats that foraged the area—St. Patrick's was barren and dry.

An equally plausible theory was that rainfall coming from the East became stalled over the mountain range, thoroughly soaking Long Ground, and almost none reached the southwestern part of the island.

Because of her knowledge of the local plant life, Katy was a joy to have along on our hike. As we neared the falls, the foliage grew lusher and included heliconia. Katy tried to pick one to give to me, but the stems were extremely tough, and since none of us was carrying a knife, she found a solution: She broke a bottle a careless hiker had discarded and sawed the stem with that.

Two young Americans and their Montserratian guide plus two other couples were the only ones we saw along the trail. And when we reached the falls, we were alone. Wanting to take a picture of a giant philodendron leaf to show the size, we posed Katy holding one next to her head. Ever the clown, she covered half of herself with the leaf and, then, giggling, unmasked.

As we walked back to the car, Katy spotted a billy goat with his harem. None of the goats was tied and could have been expected to run away. But Katy talked to billy, and he came right over, smelling just as ripe as I'd always heard male goats do. The woman running a nearby snack shop said this particular goat was brought to Montserrat from Redonda, a tiny, wild, uninhabited island just off Nevis. Everybody fed the big billy cake and bread; that's why he was tame, the woman said.

I imagine the billy became a resident of Montserrat to increase the gene pool, which tended to become smaller and smaller without an infusion of outsiders. The same was true of people; the island's elite went to college off-island and found spouses there.

We also made arrangements with Katy to take a hike into Tree Top, a former sugar plantation in the mountains near her home in Harris'. A ruin for many years, the Tree Top estate was being reconstructed by a Montserratian businessman and was planned to serve as a little resort for the newly hatched field of eco-tourism. The new owner of the property was building a lodge, and he had plans to rent out five-acre plots for farming.

What was so appealing about the area was its wild jungle look. As we walked, we saw huge mahogany trees, banana plants, giant ferns and stands of ginger, exotic with waxy, deep green leaves and maroon flowers like big brushes. I liked the strangler figs best. They put down roots from high up in the branches and, over the years, created a curtain of tree.

The ruins of the estate house were barely visible from the road that had recently been bulldozed through the jungle so construction equipment could reach the site. But you could pinpoint where the ruin was by the royal palms which grew tall beside it, planted there long ago. The year before, when we hiked into the area, there was only a footpath, and the jungle was so thick we never did see the ruins of what was a mansion back in the 1700s or early 1800s.

Just above the house was a small pond where Katy said other farmers used to bring their cattle to drink. They came for the fresh water from as far away as Tuitt's and Bramble villages, she said. The estate also had a cistern, which people from Harris' village used. Katy said she often carried water from the cistern in a bucket on her head. This was before Harris' had a "pipe."

We knew that the "East" was historically an island outpost, but we'd never realized to what extent. Katy, who was in a reminiscing mood as we explored the Tree Top ruins, said when she was a child and until the 1950s, lanterns on posts served as the street lights in Harris', and news was tacked up on a bulletin board under glass. (Ed and I saw news spread the same way when we visited the then-Soviet Union in 1988.) Katy said urgent news was read by a "town crier" who rang a bell to let everyone know he had a message, a method still in use in the 1940s and 1950s.

Interesting events involving "culture" did take place on the island. During the Christmas season one year there was a talent show, put on by young members of the Rotary Club. It was held in the Shamrock Cinema, which was badly damaged in Hurricane Hugo, but, even so, was still being used for various special events on the island. The movie theater in the vast building was defunct, killed perhaps by cable television and the VCR.

Vic Henry, who sat next to me on the upholstered seats, said the theater used to have second-run movies Monday and Tuesday evenings, with what he called the "honky matinee" on Monday afternoons. Since many of the expats were older and some just plain old and didn't like to drive at night, the honky matinee was a concession to them.

On the weekends, Henry said, the fare was Bruce Lee and other kung fu films, much appreciated by Montserratians. We had earlier noticed that Antigua TV, the only station we could get on our television, also featured so many martial arts movies that the casual observer would notice and wonder why. I still don't know.

Talent at the Rotary Club show was quite good, we thought, what we could understand of the dialect and what we could hear over the clatter of large fans used to cool the building. We stayed until after the eight contestants, wearing clothing fit for a fancy party, introduced themselves and, later, performed the numbers they'd been practicing. When 10:45 p.m. came, however, with more program to come, we left. Perhaps we were beginning to understand that it was only older white people who went to bed early.

Festivals, concerts and contests marked all the seasons: harvest, Christmas, Easter, the end of school, the beginning of school. The bigger ones, such as the Christmas dance contest we attended, were held in Sturge Park, the island's cricket and parade ground. Contestants came from St. Kitts, Antigua, the British Virgin Islands and Montserrat.

We had been warned that events in the Caribbean sometimes did not start on time, but we assumed this meant they would be 10 minutes late. Although the dance contest was advertised as starting at 8 p.m., it was not until 9 p.m. that the competition actually began. In the United States, the audience would have started clapping at 8:15, and some would have stormed the box office by 8:30.

Members of the audience seemed to know the show would be late; many didn't show up at the park until 8:30. And they didn't sit down then, preferring to mill around the little booths where beer, soft drinks and snacks were sold. We bought some unbuttered popcorn in a little sack and sat down in one of the rows of ubiquitous plastic lawn chairs to eat and to wait. And we waited. And we waited.

Another lesson we were learning: Go with the flow. There wasn't anything we could do to speed up the production, so we might as well enjoy the scenery, the silhouette of the mountains to our left and the cruise ship at anchor to our right, lit up like a Christmas tree.

Once the dancing started, it was obvious the judges would have a very hard time, as the performances were so varied. The British Virgin Islands troupe performed a traditional folk dance, for example, and the Antigua group favored hip hop/rap. The Montserrat team, hastily put together and called "The Dynamics," was the hit of the show. In their first number, combining gymnastics and break dancing, they were "Jumbies," the dead come to life. When they first entered the stage, the dancers' costumes were cardboard boxes shaped like coffins, and they had skeletons painted on their clothes. The crowd went wild.

Intermission acts also were well received. An obese woman, who called herself "Slick Chick," rap danced, and the "Oriole String Band," six men who played tin can maracas, banjo, guitar, harmonica and a PVC pipe for low notes, entertained with calypso and folk music. At 11 p.m., the judging not yet done, we headed home. We encountered only one other car as we drove to the Eastside of the island. The next day, we learned that "The Dynamics" from Montserrat had won the contest.

It was important not to think too much about time. One festival week, even though we had to drive across the mountains to Sturge Park in the rain, we opted not to start out until we should have arrived. Holding ourselves back from arriving at the designated time of 2 p.m. was hard.

On the way, we stopped beside a crowd of three women and several children waiting in the rain for a ride, knowing we wouldn't be able to squeeze everyone into our little car. We wanted to be helpful, however, so let them sort out the situation. We were amazed when the women said they would ride and told the older kids to find their own way into town. The kids complained, but only a little.

It had obviously been raining quite a while in Sturge Park, because the sound equipment was covered with blue plastic. Although it was 2:40 by the time we arrived, the afternoon's entertainment hadn't started yet. We sat for three hours waiting, during which time people kept streaming in until the grandstand was about half full.

The show started with steel drum music by groups of children from two villages, all performing on the field while we sat in the open-air stands. About the time they started to play, the skies opened up on us all. In the tropics, rainstorms do not start gently, and they do not end slowly. Everything is abrupt and there usually is considerable wind. On this day, it was 75 degrees, so nobody minded getting wet.

Soon a parade of children and adults in bright costumes marched into the park and paused at the edge of what was to be the stage area. When the rain didn't abate after several minutes, the announcer said the dancers wanted to perform anyway. The first group was whip dancers from Harris', men and boys who produced their version of what long-ago slaves saw through the windows of their masters' elegant homes. They were followed by a troupe of "Junior Jumbies," all trained and outfitted by the Henrys' daughter Barb.

Many aspects of this festival were related to the spirits of the dead. All of the children in Barb's troupe, for example, wore headdresses made of fluorescent fabric, and each wore a mask, symbolizing jumbies (ghosts).

When you considered that every fabric, feather, mask and pair of bicycle pants the dancers wore had to come from poorly stocked shops on the island plus mail order, you realized that outfitting a whole group of performers was a miracle.

Barb's own costume included a peacock tail wired in an arc with "feathers" of the same fluorescent fabric topped by a plume. On her back, she wore an entire skeleton, which dangled and wiggled as she walked. These elaborate costumes, which were worn for Mardi Gras-like celebrations, often had to be welded together. Rondo, who ran the Texaco station near Harris', was her sponsor and fabricated the superstructure of her costume.

The show went on, despite continuing rain, and included a group of dancers from Antigua, the Oriole String Band and a group of "Junior Calypsonians," most of whom couldn't sing but deserved prizes for effort, nonetheless.

WHAT IS CALYPSO?

An Afro-Caribbean musical form, calypso was born in Trinidad and Tobago in the early 20th century, but has roots going back to the 18th century and the slave trade. Calypso is known as "the voice of the people" because lyrics tend to be political—challenging government and complaining about social ills.

Songs are usually written by the performers.

This music is often accompanied by steel drums, also called "pans." Because some officials in the past thought steel drums and other percussion instruments promoted violence, such instruments were forbidden in about 1881 but reappeared in the 1930s.

When we were on Montserrat, pans were quite well accepted, and children even had pan classes at school. There were competitions to see who the best players were. Pan makers, who used empty oil drums to create their instruments, were true artisans.

Despite lack of training, money for costumes and pushy mothers, the children astounded us with their stage presence and their drive to excel, even at pre-school ages. Why? We never saw a whiny, nervous child or an irritable stage mother. Likewise, we never saw a reluctant performer. We finally decided that this complete lack of worry about the outcome came from the fact that most children on Montserrat knew they were loved unconditionally and that this love came not just from their immediate families but from their entire village.

(Children who misbehaved were corrected by any adult who happened to be on the scene. Kids knew what was expected. And so did the grown-ups.)

White expatriates had their own entertainment. One night we attended a performance of *Harvey* by the Readers' Theatre with Paul Mabry, the Bethel Church's choir director, as the lead, Elwood P. Dowd. Paul and his wife, Adele, had lived in Spanish Point at one time before moving to the West to be near the golf club.

Those of us on the Eastside of the island didn't even know the Readers' Theatre evenings existed until I was invited to attend by Mabry. This play was read and acted in a private home. About 40 people sat on the patio and on the low wall surrounding the swimming pool to watch the play, which was staged in the couple's living room. Like many of the larger Montserrat homes, the living areas of the house opened out onto the pool deck, thus blending inside and outside.

We met an expat who operated a studio where she and two Montserratian women made pottery for the tourist trade. Her husband had come to the island many years before and had, at first, supported himself by making heavy lamps that wouldn't tip over in the wind and wind chimes of rings cut from empty wine bottles and strung together with fishing line.

Ed and I had taken ceramics classes at the Indianapolis Art League (now the Indianapolis Art Center in Indianapolis in Broad Ripple) and he was eager to continue. I was never any good at the potter's wheel; my blobs of clay tended to go whirling off the wheel or ended in a state of collapse. But I wasn't bad at glazing pots after their first firing.

Our new friend, Carmen French, said the pottery that came from her studio was all made from soupy clay poured into molds. Her two employees, Cissie and Nicole, poured the large pineapples, pelicans and bowls that looked like shells. They also poured large platters and utilitarian bowls. Then they trimmed their creations, dried and fired them.

Mrs. French, who took the half-finished pieces home to apply glazes and do the final firing, said she had a potter's wheel that no one was using and invited Ed to try his hand. So he made pots on the wheel, and I glazed them. It was an activity we could do together, an artistic endeavor that was very satisfying. After a few months, Ed and I had a backlog, which Carmen let us sell in her shop.

The best thing about going to the pottery studio was not getting our hands into the gooey clay, but the chance to talk with Cissie and Nicole. They were full of information about the island, information we couldn't get anywhere else. For example, they told us that some people in their neighborhood used to make money by breaking up rocks and selling them to the Department of Public Works to use on the roads. When the "crusher"—the local term for the quarry that was located a few miles north of us in the East—was established, this method of making money was no longer available for ordinary Montserratians. "We used to get EC $30 or about $10 US for a truckload," Cissie said. I had heard this rock-busting story on the Eastside of the island, too.

The pottery studio was a stone building used in some capacity during the sugar cane plantation era. As such, the floors were earthen, and there was no toilet on the premises. Cissie and Nicole had to walk up the road to a restaurant to use the restroom. Walls in the building were about 18 inches thick, and windows were small and few. It was kind of a primitive place to work.

One day, at about noon, the women produced a fish from a plastic bag and said it was going to be their lunch. Seeing no charcoal burner or hot plate, I wondered how a stiff fish was going to turn into a meal. But then they showed us how they planned to wad up several sheets of an old *New York Times*, a precious commodity on the island, it seemed, and plop the fish on top. Then, they would set the newspaper on fire with kitchen matches. When the paper burned down, the fish would be cooked enough to eat—to their taste at least. Nicole told me, "This is the Montserratian way." A typical beach picnic on the island, she said, was a roasted breadfruit, a freshly caught fish and a "lime squash," made of lime juice, sugar and water.

When we knew them really well, Nicole said she wanted to ask "a personal question." Was it true, like most black people think, that white people have inheritances from their parents. "Some people do, but some don't," Ed told her. Nicole said there was some jealousy over this belief, whether true or not, because a lot of black people were having money problems. But they themselves might be at least partly at fault, she said. "A lot of black people never have anything because they have too many children."

She and Cissie then wanted to know if I had worked full-time outside the home, and I said that, yes, I had, for 14 years, but not until after our two children were nearly grown. Nicole said she had heard that white people drink a lot and party a lot and have fully stocked bars in their houses. I told her we didn't drink alcoholic beverages at all and had only one bottle of rum in the house, and that was to cook with. She seemed very surprised.

I could understand where she got that idea. I heard a white man in the bank just that morning say to another, much too loudly, "Great party last night, wasn't it?"

Nicole said she knew for white people who entertained it wasn't uncommon for people to have 20 or 30 to their house for drinks and dinner. With the price of food on the island 60 percent higher than in the States, that would be a budget buster and a subject to marvel at for local people struggling to put food on the table.

Bethel Methodist Church survived Hurricane Hugo in 1989. But the steeple and roof sustained damage. It couldn't withstand the volcano, however.

Hurricane Hugo turned Montserrat into a vast junkyard. The remains of people's lives littered the ground. For weeks in some areas, there was no electricity or running water. We arrived on the island not long after this hurricane.

The War Memorial and the office of the treasury brightened up downtown Plymouth. This square was the scene of the Christmas carol sing.

I tried for a long time to tame my favorite goat "Nice Girl." Tasty leaves served as teaching tools.

Our "as is" furniture was adequate, but I improved its look with new upholstery.

Swimming in the pool with palm fronds gently blowing in the breeze was the highlight of my day. If I stood up, I could see Antigua 27 miles away.

Ed was the "candyman." When he showed up with rainfall tree cuttings to share, the goats came running.

Sunny Jim, cozying down in one of our island chairs.

This snow around our Indianapolis home shows why we loved Montserrat.

11
TIME TO BE HOLY

For many, life on Montserrat revolved around church, and there were many to choose from. Methodist missionaries particularly had been active on the island. There were at least seven separate congregations of Methodists. In addition, Pentecostal, Apostolic, Baptist, Catholic, Seventh-day Adventist and Anglican were represented.

On our first Sunday as "belongers," the term used to identify property owners on the island, we walked up the hill to the Methodist Church to attend the worship service. It was convenient, and we had been members of a large Methodist church "up north" since the late '50s.

Wishard and Sunny were well behaved and well acclimated to our house, so we left them at home. We knew they would both be asleep when we returned, since both were too old by then to get into trouble.

There was no way to live in Spanish Point and not be aware of the large Methodist Church with the tall spire. The Bethel church bells were rung on our first Sunday morning at 8:45 a.m. although the service didn't start until 9:30. The bell ringer, the sexton of the church, rode around our area on a donkey during the week, checking on his sheep and goats. He was just as devoted to his bell ringing on Sundays, as we later learned.

Some religious groups still came to the island to proselytize. Jehovah's Witnesses, for example, were actively recruiting in Plymouth, and on one occasion a revival tent was set up in Spanish Point. The month-long series was scheduled to take place after dinner, when a van containing a handful of people, both black and white, pulled up at the tent. Maybe 10 more people, mostly senior citizens from the villages, meandered down, too.

Over the course of the month, I passed by on numerous occasions, sometimes just to see what was going on. The preacher seemed to use maps and charts, to which he pointed with a long stick. The "congregation" sat on hard benches. The program looked boring, and from what I could see, the people thought it was boring, too. If the leaders of the revival knew how many of the people in their congregation were no doubt illiterate and couldn't make sense out of a map, perhaps they would have used some other tactic.

In a farming community like ours, church and everything else were all mixed up. One Sunday our first winter, we chased a cow that had jumped into our yard. Then we immediately trudged up the hill to church—too out of breath to hustle, although we were late. The preacher that Sunday was a layman, who wore what I would call a short-sleeved, Nehru-collared suit. He was a bit more charismatic than the staid Methodists were prepared to accept.

It wasn't that he didn't include in the service some old hymns by Charles and John Wesley and by Isaac Watts—Methodist mainstays all—it was just that he added some with a definitely more lively beat. Trying to rev up the congregation, he strode down to the altar rail, singing as he went, clapping his hands and trying to entice the congregation to do the same.

They refused; in fact, they were not amused. When he asked them to stand and sing, some flatly refused. One woman, decked out in a floating, pink chiffon dress, stood, but after several verses with more to come, she sat down. The preacher became agitated and as much as told the congregation they were dead. They were not amused by that either. Yet, no one fidgeted. Children didn't cry or complain. They just sat woodenly with their parents, who seemed carved from dark wood.

But the decorum finally was broken. While a parishioner read the week's announcements—where the women's club was meeting and who would be doing church cleanup the next Saturday—a two-year-old boy with his hair in little braids and his long pants held up with suspenders toddled up to the front and climbed the steps to the dais where the altar was. The preacher sat in a chair on a platform several steps above this lower level, and the baby carefully climbed up there, too, not saying anything, nor crying.

His mother or grandmother said nothing and made no move to grab him and take him back to his pew. After exploring near the pulpit, he carefully climbed down the steps, backwards as babies universally are taught to do, and wandered off to the back of the church. A couple of adults chuckled. The preacher smiled, but said nothing. And soon he began his closing prayer. The benediction came nearly two hours after the service started.

Because there weren't enough ministers to go around to each and every Methodist Church, some of the services were lay-led, and sometimes the preachers were church bureaucrats. In my observation, the latter were long on words, but short on content. One of them was particularly adept at stringing platitudes together, all the while taking off and putting on a pair of half glasses. To keep myself occupied, I counted how many times the glasses went off and on.

During our tenure on the island, we heard him preach several times. Watching him was more interesting than listening to his sermons. After I had joined the choir, I confided in Margaret Joseph, who was president of the congregation, head of the choir and a long-time teacher in the Montserrat schools, that Ed and I had agreed to count the numbers of times the superintendent patted his glasses or took them off. At first, when he had done this, we thought it was because they were half-lens reading glasses, and he didn't need them to see unless he was looking at his notes. But he eventually acquired new bifocals, which he wore all the time. Yet, his old habit remained.

We also told Margaret that we had made plans to count how many times he said "My dear friends" and "brothers and sisters" during the sermon. She seemed a bit shocked. We were going to be busy with dual counting.

I couldn't look at Ed during the service, too afraid I would laugh indecorously. The reverend racked up only five "brothers and sister" and two "my dear friends" and took off his glasses only twice. But he adjusted them 49 times. We told Angie Jones about the count; she did not seem amused either.

On a Sunday during the Christmas season, this bureaucrat wore a long black robe and a clerical collar, even though it was hot. The congregation, dressed in clothing appropriate for a wedding or the Queen's garden party, never fidgeted, but a cow mooing just outside the church door seemed to add just the right touch.

Many of the women of the church talked about "covenant Sunday," which we didn't understand, but we decided to go to church out of curiosity instead of religious fervor. The purpose of the service, which, it turned out, was held in Methodist churches all over the island, was to provide an opportunity for parishioners to "recovenant" their lives to Jesus. There were hints that this service would take all morning, if not more.

Mostly, that was because three congregations were meeting together for this event —Bethel, Long Ground and Harris'. This arrangement was necessary because the island's new minister at the time, the young Quentin Plum, could not make it to three churches in one morning.

By actual count, there were 10 hymns on the program, and each had at least six verses, all of which we sang. Then there was the sermon, which went on and on and on and had a lot to do with sin. I didn't listen very carefully, but most of the parishioners seemed to. One very large woman wearing a big, floppy hat and a polka-dotted dress said "Praise Jesus" and "Hallelujah" many times during the sermon. We were told after the service that she wasn't from OUR church.

After the minister finally quit preaching, he conducted an altar call, which I hadn't seen since I was a child. About 30 women, most of them middle-aged or older, and one man came forward to rededicate themselves to the Lord. The woman who had been saying "Praise Jesus" really got noisy then, weeping and wailing. A couple of people in the congregation laughed out loud at this and one woman covered her face in embarrassment.

The service didn't last as long as I feared—only 2 1/2 hours—after which there was to be a brunch at the manse, the structure on which Ed had been asked to concentrate his efforts after the hurricane. He helped reconstruct the porch.

While we were eating, Paul Mabry, the choir director, asked Ed and me if we'd be willing to help out by singing in the choir. Ed was aghast at the idea, saying he was no singer, but I decided to say yes. I had sung in church choirs when I was a teen-ager and thought it might be fun and a good way to meet people.

The next week, with some trepidation, I attended my first choir practice. I wasn't worried about the social aspect, but I was scared to death about driving the car up the mountain—even what amounted to a few blocks—to the church and parking it in the tiny lot. This was especially worrisome for me because on Montserrat we drove on the left, and the steering wheel was on the right.

Paul, his wife Adele and I turned out to be the only white people in the choir. Adele sometimes played the keyboard we were using in lieu of an organ, which was destroyed in Hurricane Hugo. The minister had asked that we learn a cantata which had been written in Jamaica for the dedication of the new organ, which was on order. Sharon Jones also played the keyboard on Sunday mornings.

The cantata had difficult rhythms for anyone without a lot of prior musical experience; it also was atonal. I thought it was far above the capabilities of the tiny little choir. But it surely wasn't my place to say so.

We sang all the hymns for Sunday morning and some warm-up exercises with which Paul Mabry was attempting to coerce the women into forming round tones without screeching on the high notes. Then one of the choir members introduced me to everybody.

And as we were leaving the church, a young woman, Alicia Sweeney, came up to me shyly, took my hand and said, "Welcome to our choir." She told me she lived in Harris,' which was between 2 and 2 1/2 miles up the mountain from the Bethel Church. I don't believe she was related to Evelyn Sweeney, but she might have been.

Female choir members routinely tested the patience of the director by being late to rehearsal. It was even more maddening when they were late serially and waltzed in as if nothing were amiss. Once there, they sang at the top of their lungs, off-key and screeching.

When the screeching grew intolerable, Mabry would stop the rehearsal and have us do vocalizing exercises up and down the scale. The ladies immediately quieted down while singing "Ah, ah, ah, ah, ah and ee, ee, ee, ee, ee,"and their tone quality improved. But when we returned to singing the anthem for Sunday morning, they started screeching the high notes again. In addition to tardiness, the women were inconsistent in showing up at all. Some of those who came to choir practice on a Thursday didn't show up on Sunday morning, and some of those who hadn't been to choir practice on Thursday showed up to sing for the Sunday service.

One of the stalwarts of the church, but not a member of the choir, was Edith Myers, the postmistress. But she seemed to be somehow connected to us all because she always sat on a folding chair behind the choir loft, out of sight of everyone in the congregation. She usually wore a silky print dress, a curly wig to cover her braids and a large hat. Maybe she just didn't want to be seen. Maybe she wanted to be close to the outdoor toilet, which was just out the door behind her.

She confided in us one day that she had been invited out to the royal yacht *Brittania*. Prince Philip was going to come to the island for an official visit a few weeks after this and a few select persons were apparently going to make a visit to the yacht. This was the first I had heard we were going to have a royal visitation. I told her that perhaps she would get a title and be hereinafter called "Lady." Margaret Joseph said she already called Mrs. Myers "Miss Edithanna," so she already had a title.

Margaret, who had her hand in nearly everything that happened in the church, announced after one choir practice that she had done a bad thing, and she giggled behind her hand. This terribly bad thing was that she had purchased fabric for choir robes. We had talked about how nice it would be to have robes, but the subject was dropped. This announcement came as a bit of a shock to many of the choir members.

By buying 60 yards, Margaret said, she was able to get 13 Eastern Caribbean dollar-a-meter fabric for EC $7 a meter. We each owed her EC $60 or $20 US. Adele Mabry said she would draft a pattern and give everyone instructions on how to sew a robe. As was usual, the women sat quietly and didn't say anything. That could have meant approval or disapproval. When questioned, one of the women said she didn't know how to sew. Nobody volunteered to make an extra robe. Since I had a sewing machine, I figured I might be called upon to make more than my own, which I was willing to do within reason. But I wasn't keen on making 15 robes, so I didn't say anything either.

Non-response seemed to be a cultural thing—perhaps begun during slave times when speaking up might cause trouble. Non-expression as a coping mechanism probably served the people well. What was my excuse?

I wondered what level of desperation was at work when a certain old man was asked to preach on a Sunday. Or was a joke being played on the congregation? At least nobody went to sleep, which I suppose was the goal of many a minister—to keep the congregation alert for what was coming next.

The old man started off by saying that Jesus created the world and everything in it. And then he said a lot of people opposed Jesus, which was true, and even had guns trained on him from the hills, which wasn't true because gunpowder wasn't invented until the 14th century. Oh, yes, and the old man stated unequivocally that Jesus spoke Greek.

While preaching, he strode around the dais with a microphone in his hand. I think he had been watching televangelists a little too much. Some of the members of the choir must have heard him before, as they sat sort of bent over, their hands covering their faces. Others talked among themselves during the service, so I guess they didn't buy everything he said.

So why was he allowed to be a lay minister in the Methodist church, since he didn't follow any Methodist ideas I ever heard of? Because he was the father of one of the top government officials, that's why. One of the choir members told me after the service that he always told "jokes" during the services he led, and she just laughed them off.

When we had houseguests, we didn't always attend the Methodist church. We took one couple to the Anglican church in Harris'; they were Episcopalians in the United States. A Mr. Duberry, a large black man the color of ebony wood, introduced himself when we entered the church and sat with us so as to help us with the liturgy. Mainly, we needed to know which of three possible books was used in different parts of the service.

This was high church—I like to say it was "more Catholic than Catholic"—with lots of incense and the ringing of bells. There was no kneeling during the service, but parishioners did cross themselves and genuflected before they took their seats.

At one point in the service, everyone who had celebrated a birthday in the past week came to the altar to be blessed by the priest. Then the congregation sang the "Happy Birthday" song. And the contact between parishioners and priest didn't stop there or with the Eucharist. Children didn't take Communion with the adults, but afterward, they all were asked to come to the altar to be blessed. Even mothers with tiny, sleeping babies went forward to have the priest lay his hands on them and say a few words.

The next day we took our visitors to the village of Judy Piece to see the Methodist church, which had been totally blown away by Hurricane Hugo, but rebuilt by parishioners and work groups from the United States. Like many other churches on the island, the new building was poured concrete with windows of colored glass.

Judy Piece is high up on the mountainside on the north side of the island, and it was thus easy to see why the fierce winds of Hugo had done so much damage. From the churchyard, you could see the Atlantic in the East and, by whirling around, the Caribbean in the

West. Sheep were tethered in the small, windswept graveyard beside the church, the better to take advantage of the tall grass growing there. A ewe became frantic when we walked between her and her baby, which was not tied. The mother lunged against her rope and bleated.

That had been a day for confrontations with sheep. Earlier, a tiny black lamb, probably born the day before, judging from the fact that a large piece of umbilical cord was hanging from its tummy, was bleating pitifully near the fence behind our house. As it was too young to have any fear of humans, I was able to thread my way through the bushes and undergrowth behind the fence, pick it up and carry it, kicking wildly, to the road out front, where, I hoped, its mother would find it.

The lamb couldn't have weighed more than three pounds. I wondered how long it had been without food.

Not all religious people expressed their piety in a church. Ed was repairing a gutter on our house one day when he heard what he thought was a religious radio station, played at full blast. I had heard it, too, from inside the house. Judging from the direction of the sound, it came from a spot down the hill from us.

Soon, as we stood still, we could see movement, particularly a waving of arms, and realized that the sound was coming from a man standing on a rock and preaching to the morning air and whoever might be listening. The area of Spanish Point from which he preached was nearly uninhabited.

From what I could gather, he was talking about power and God's judgment and sin, and interspersed with the words, which we could hear clearly only some of the time, he sang gospel hymns at the top of his lungs. No one walked over to listen to the preaching, and, likewise, no one called the police or tried to stop him. Pretty soon, he climbed down from the rock on which he was standing and wandered away. Later, William told us that the man, who lived in Harris' when he wasn't preaching, visited all the villages around the island. One day he became convinced he'd been called by the Lord and that this was his mission, to preach about sin and salvation to whoever might possibly hear him. William's take on this was that one should never question the motives or the sanity of a Godly man.

Margaret Joseph made unilateral decisions about what the choir would wear on Sundays. One week, for example, she told us on Thursday that we were to wear all white. I told them all I had nothing white in my wardrobe—a statement they found hard to believe. But it was true. I am such a slob that I decided years ago that white was not practical for me, no matter where I went. I did not waver from this self-imposed restriction, despite the fact that nearly every tourist visiting the Caribbean wore white shorts or slacks.

On Montserrat, I learned, white was worn to church on special Sundays and also, sometimes, to funerals. Otherwise, mourners were supposed to wear black. I didn't have anything black in my wardrobe either.

We had heard that the upcoming Sunday service was going to last five hours and include lunch, a prayer service and then group discussions. Although Ed rarely wore his watch, he repaired the broken band with duct tape so he would know when his limit of 1 1/2 hours had elapsed. At that point, he intended to walk out.

To prepare for the service, I put on my old standby blue skirt and blue and white striped blouse, the closest I could come to the prescribed outfit de jour. Since I was singing in the choir, I didn't know when escaping the endless service would be propitious, if ever, for me. I told Ed I hoped not to have to stay from 9 a.m. until noon, but, I added, "I'll meet you at home sometime."

When the choir assembled in the tiny and nearly airless sacristy just moments before the service, the minister, Quentin Plum, said he'd intended to have a 15-minute hymn sing at 8:45 a.m., before the service began, but that none of us had shown up early enough. He didn't realize he was lucky to have a choir of any size by 9 a.m. Many singers walked slowly in and climbed the steps to the choir loft, totally unconcerned, even though they were ten or fifteen minutes late. Or more.

Quentin had planned the service so there were seven hymns plus a sung canticle, and we sang all verses of everything at a speed which could only be described as funereal. There were also several long readings from the new prayer book, which was being officially launched at the service and had been designed by the Methodist Church specifically for the Caribbean. Then followed interminable announcements from our church's lay leader.

The preacher of the day was not Quentin, but an import I'd never seen or heard before. He preached on how the devil gets a hold on people. A first step, he said, was for people to start criticizing—the length of the service, the number of hymns and the minister's message. (He must have overheard Ed and me talking.) Criticizing leads to cutting church, which is also the devil's work, he said. Cutting church, he insisted, leads to failing to attend altogether. Ed said later that if a minister ever said such a thing directly to him, he would reply, "Well, maybe the devil is getting you to make the service so long it drives people away."

The church was packed for this dressing-down, and Quentin also had planned to have Communion, during which communicants would walk down front, as many as the altar rail would hold at a time, and kneel down. This would take a long time, I knew, and the choir was to sing additional hymns as background to the ritual. When the choir was invited to the Communion rail, which was before the rest of the congregation came, I slipped out the back door. For all anyone knew, I had to use the restroom.

Later, I learned that the Mabrys had made their exit at the same time. Adele and Sharon had been dividing the keyboard player's duties, making this possible. Adele and Paul had more on their minds that morning than attending a long and boring service; they were due to attend a memorial service on the fifth green of the golf course for a friend who had died—there or elsewhere. I didn't ask.

Adele Mabry, as she said she would, drafted a pattern for the choir robes and had even cut out the pieces, which she brought to a choir practice. She asked who was going to make her own, and not one hand went up. Adele told the women (there were no men attending the rehearsal) that she wasn't taking any of the robe pieces back home. She then asked who could get someone to make their robes if they couldn't. At first, there was no response here either, but finally she was able to worm out of the women the fact that they all knew someone who could sew. This meant that Adele and I were both off the hook.

If she hadn't stood firm, I believe she and I would have ended up making all the robes. In a way, I felt sorry for the women because this chore was foisted off on them. They had no input as to whether they would have robes or not, although they had long talked about having them. Most were probably content to wear their normal, Sunday-morning dresses.

Evelyn Sweeney, who lived close to us in Spanish Point, did take cut-out pieces for her robe, but she was having difficulty putting them together and gave me a call. Since I had prepared the written instructions based on the prototype robe that Adele made, I guess I was the logical one to help. Evelyn was embarrassed, but, she said, she never used patterns. Thus, she was having a hard time following written directions.

So I walked up the hill to her house to help. She had a dress she was making laid out on her bed, and I asked her how she could put together something so complicated, set-in sleeves and a peplum at the waist, without instructions. She said she just started cutting and sewing.

Just then, Margaret stopped by on her way home from school, where she taught English. She had already made several robes, no doubt for the people who didn't raise their hands or who indicated they knew somebody who could sew for them, and she offered to finish Evelyn's robe, too.

The two women had quite a discussion, then, about hats. They wanted to wear hats with their robes and were wondering if they could buy some all alike. I, meanwhile, kept quiet, but hoped they weren't serious. I hadn't worn a hat except to play tennis, perhaps, since the 1960s when young women in the States largely stopped dressing up. No more hats and gloves and hose for shopping down-town. No more garter belts and girdles and hose with seams. Yeah!

One of the women suggested that perhaps we could make hats to go with the collars which were going to be made to go with the robes. These collars would be changed for various occasions, Margaret said. We would each have a set of blue, red, green, gold and purple collars. I wondered who would make all of those.

They asked me what I thought about the hats, and I told them I wasn't the one to ask as I never wore them. They seemed surprised.

12
GOING UPSCALE

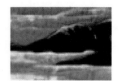

The major reason for having the robes was that soon (we didn't know when) the new organ to replace the one that was destroyed in the hurricane would be delivered. And then church would be as it was supposed to be in proper communities.

So the excitement was palpable the evening in March when we arrived for choir practice and there the new organ was. Unfortunately, we soon found out, the organ had some kind of glitch, as a terrible sound, like a crack of thunder, emanated from it whenever keys were pressed. Adele quickly turned off the instrument and asked Freddy Connor, one of the male mainstays of the Bethel Church, to walk over to the manse, several hundred feet away, to summon the Allen organ representative, who was on island to oversee the organ's installation.

(Freddy might or might not have been a relative of Katy Connor's husband.)

In the meantime, however, we had to practice with our old electronic keyboard, the same one on which Sharon and Adele had been playing since shortly after the 1989 hurricane. Although tones could be adjusted to resemble those of a real organ, the sound couldn't be amplified enough that it could be heard throughout the cavernous church.

The organ dedication was slated for March 28, in only 10 days. On the Saturday before that date, I sewed hooks and eyes on my robe, so I would be ready for the procession on Sunday. It would be the choir's first formally dressed appearance. We were to enter singing Beethoven's "Ode to Joy" from his 9th symphony, very impressive for a bunch of amateurs. When I arrived at church for the morning service, however, Paul broke the news: the organ dedication scheduled for that afternoon had to be postponed. He said the reason was "top secret."

Instead of the choir, the women's club sang the anthem. Several members of the choir were also in the women's club, and I noted they hadn't learned anything from Paul. They screeched as much as ever.

Margaret gathered a committee to help her make velour covers for the organ and new curtains for the altar rail. They had also decorated the wall behind the pulpit with purchased flower arrangements, all in preparation for the organ dedication, which now was going to be held during the regularly scheduled service on Palm Sunday.

Paul said the dedication couldn't be Palm Sunday afternoon because the Cork Hill Methodist Church on the Westside was planning to dedicate its new building then, and all the Methodists on the island were invited. The former building was a victim of Hurricane Hugo.

Nothing was going right. Adele noticed that the batteries on the Yamaha keyboard were low, so she announced she would play only the first chord of each measure, hoping to preserve enough sound to last for the whole service. Angie Jones slipped out and drove up the hill to her house to pick up more batteries. Evelyn Sweeney did, too, but when she returned, we had to tell her they were the wrong size. Sharon Jones changed the batteries, with some clattering, while the minister was preaching.

Originally, Paul had said we would have an extra choir practice after the regular Sunday morning service. I thought since the organ dedication was postponed, we'd not have to practice. He decided we needed to.

I concurred when I heard we were going to sing not one but two songs at the dedication—"Oh, Give Thanks," which had time changes from 3/4 to 6/8 to 12/8 and "Peter on the Sea, Sea, Sea," which had screwy timing and everyone singing at different times. Both were large challenges, particularly for a choir made up of people who couldn't read music.

After the rehearsal, which made me fear a disaster was in the making, Paul told me the reason the organ dedication had to be postponed. He asked me not to tell any of the Montserratians because they would be upset. Sometime after Thursday evening when the choir practiced, the organ stopped working completely. He said it would be a miracle if the Allen representative, who had returned to

St. Croix, could come to Montserrat and fix the instrument before Palm Sunday.

Paul came over to our house on the next choir practice day to see if Ed and he could make contact with a brother in Canada by amateur radio. He told us then that the organ still was not repaired. MONLEC (Montserrat Electric Company) had sent a crew out to check on the wiring in the church, and a new circuit board had been ordered to replace one dropped in transit. The organ dedication was going to be cancelled again. This meant going to plan C, which might be Maundy Thursday, after or during the regularly scheduled Holy Week service. Failing that, he said, "who knows" when the organ would be dedicated? For what good, after all, was an organ which didn't work?

I was aware that the Mabrys had planned to go "bock-up" to Canada right after Easter. It was possible Paul would not be on the island to conduct the special music we had been rehearsing since January.

The organ still was not repaired by Palm Sunday because the part that would supposedly do the trick had not arrived. More than likely, we could not have a dedication on Maundy Thursday either. Even so, Margaret announced that the choir would practice Tuesday evening during Holy Week, in order to be ready in case the miraculous repair occurred.

This was all very confusing, especially because the Maundy Thursday service was originally supposed to be a "circuit-wide" affair held at the Methodist Church in Judy Piece and not at Bethel. Somehow everybody would have to get the word that the place of the service had been changed. With a newspaper coming out only once a week, on Friday, and irregular reception of Zed Jay Bee, the island's radio station, I didn't know how this would be possible.

Word of mouth was quite efficient to spread gossip on a small island, so perhaps I was being unduly pessimistic. After the Palm Sunday service, Margaret announced to the choir that we would be wearing our robes on Easter Sunday, regardless of whether the organ was to be dedicated or not.

On Tuesday, she called to tell me the organ was repaired and that we were going to have the dedication on Maundy Thursday at 7 p.m. Paul was unable to lead the rehearsal that night, so we were to assemble at 6 p.m. on Thursday, just prior to the dedication service, to go over our music. We should wear our robes.

When I got off the phone, Ed said the organ needed a shake-out period before it was exhibited to the whole circuit. Oh, well. A bit later that day, the dedication was announced on Zed Jay Bee.

I couldn't imagine why some of our expat friends never listened to the local radio station. How else would you find out that a prominent man had died, leaving to mourn "friends too numerous to mention" or the fact that the Grove had two Nubian goats for sale or that the Judy Piece Methodist Church was having a choral concert? As islanders, we wanted to know these things.

Not all was calm as Maundy Thursday approached. One of the women said she didn't know how to sew, and her robe was still in pieces. I didn't really want to make it, but relented. The woman was full of complaints, which I learned when I went to pick up her unmade robe. She said she really didn't have the EC $60 which the robes cost, and she thought the robes should be provided by the church and kept there instead of being the responsibility of the individual choir members. I could see her point.

The woman also thought the robes would be too hot. I could believe that, too. I told her some of the women wanted to wear hats, even with the robes. "You must forgive them," she said. "They don't know any better." She went on and on about the mismanagement of the whole organ debacle, noting that the service was bound to last until midnight as this was a joint service, and there would be Communion in addition to the organ dedication and a sermon.

On Maundy Thursday, I showed up for the organ dedication carrying my hymnal, my robe and my purple collar, which Margaret had made. But I did not wear white or black underneath, as I had been instructed, because I had neither. I couldn't imagine why I needed to dress that way because the robe, supposedly, would cover everything. I noticed, however, that the white fabric out of which the robes were made was so thin that polka dots and prints could be plainly seen through it.

Quentin's fiancé played the organ, both for our rehearsal before the actual service began and for the real thing. Sharon, who was usually our accompanist, had no time to practice on the instrument after it was repaired and said a rehearsal wouldn't have helped as she had absolutely no knowledge as to how to play an organ. If she was the usual keyboard player and didn't know how to play an organ, then why did the church buy one? I had no answer for that.

Before the service began, I saw Katy, who was a Methodist at one time, sitting next to Ed and went over to say hello. She was wearing a red cotton dress, which, she said, "one of my customers" sent from the US. When she noted my robe, she said, "I see you can sew" and then she told me she wanted me to make her a dress.

A few days after Easter, Angie handed me a paper bag containing black velveteen and thread. "I want you to make me a jacket," she said. I protested that I could not sew without a pattern and that I'd have to get one in the States. This didn't faze her one bit. She wanted the jacket to be short-sleeved, no collar, no buttons, waist length, perfectly plain, she said. Although I was dumbfounded by this, I said, well, okay, I guess I could, maybe I could, I guess I would.

The organ dedication was such a momentous occasion that the British governor of the island attended, having been driven there in his white Land Rover with the Union Jack fluttering from a tiny flagpole on the running board. As soon as he got out of the car, the guard/driver, clad jauntily in a white tunic and hat, rolled up the flag and put a cover over it. The British governor sat down front in the church with Rupert McMillan, the island's Montserratian chief minister.

Just as the service was getting under way, I noticed that a few tiny bugs had begun to circle the fluorescent bulbs, which had been suspended on wires across the nave of the church for illumination. Ed had noticed earlier that the air was calm and wondered if this would be a perfect night for an infestation of what we laughingly called those "ibb's" (itty-bitty bugs). Before we left home, we had closed our windows and turned out the lights so we wouldn't come home to piles of dead insects. So I was not surprised when the invasion began in earnest, with thousands of the bugs flitting around the lights, falling on our music and sullying our new robes.

Saturday afternoon Margaret called to say she had another collar for me—this time red. She wanted us all to wear red collars on Easter Sunday, although we wore purple on Maundy Thursday. As far as I could tell, there was no rhyme or reason to this: nothing set out according to the liturgical year, nothing mandated by the Methodist bishop or even the local minister. What color we wore seemed to me to be based solely on her decision as to what we would—or should—wear. Margaret told the choir members that we would have another procession so we could show off our robes to those who hadn't seen them on Thursday. When Quentin learned this Easter morning, however, he vetoed the idea.

The next week, Adele turned on the organ at choir practice, and not one sound came out. We ran through our music a cappella and called it a night. The man who, a few days later, checked over the instrument, said he saw evidence of rats. The church, of course, was wide open with no glass in the windows and plenty of cracks to permit access from the outside, so rats were a possible cause. The repairman told Sharon that poison must be placed inside the organ and kept there all the time, or the wires would keep on being chewed.

The Mabrys had gone back up as they said they would. Sharon called to tell me that from then on the choir would be practicing on Saturdays. I assumed Sharon would be leading us as she was learning to play the new organ. She told me earlier, however, that she wasn't a singer, and she was sticking to it. Well, then, who WOULD lead?

With the Mabrys gone, there were bound to be changes beyond the date and time of practices. Another one, immediately apparent, was that choir members arrived late, shuffling in 15, 20 and even 30 minutes after the starting time. Several didn't bother to show up, which wasn't really any different.

The result of all this was that Sharon tried to play the organ, and we tried to sing along. That's how the rehearsal went, and it was terrible. The only direction we got was from Margaret, who told us we would be expected to wear robes at the upcoming service. Someone protested that it was awfully hot for that, but she was unconvinced.

Walter Lee, a retired teacher, took over for Paul Mabry when it became obvious we needed a director. Some of the women didn't like Walter, maybe hadn't for years, and their body language gave them away. He sang bass and could read music, which many of them couldn't. But his voice was overpowering, and theirs were thin and screechy. He went over and over the hymn the choir was singing as an anthem on Sunday morning, and the women squirmed in their seats and sighed.

13

SITUATIONS

Living in the tropics in general and Montserrat in particular created some situations. You dealt with them or you made yourself miserable. For example, our supply of water and, to a lesser extent, electricity, was unreliable. We might return home from a shopping foray into Plymouth and discover that the electricity had been off long enough that the ice cream was defrosting in the freezer. Always, when that happened, we called around to the neighbors to find out if they, too, were without power. Sometimes they were, and sometimes they weren't.

We could call the electric company, known on the island as MONLEC (Montserrat Electric Company), and two hours later no one would have come to see what the problem was. In the meantime, Ed would start the generator and at least hook up the refrigerator. Thus another problem would be temporarily solved.

Listening to the island radio station, Zed Jay Bee, every day was crucial because water and electrical outages were often announced in advance there. This way you could sometimes be ready to handle whatever utility situation came your way. For example, MONLEC would announce exactly where "line main-TAY-nance" was going to take place and during what hours. Unfortunately, it wasn't all that unusual to hear that the power would be off in Spanish Point from 8 a.m. to 4 p.m.

But sometimes the power went off without warning. Because of the salt spray from our ever-present trade winds, anything metal corroded, even though we were about 800 yards back from the water and 350 feet above sea level. I made protective covers out of old shower curtains for our computer and Ed's amateur radio. The aluminum window cranks became pitted, and the screens, which often seemed to have drops of something sticky running down them, were falling into holes. At first, we thought that was because of the age of the screens, and we thought the sticky stuff was sap from a tree. But alas, there were no trees nearby.

Somebody told us that the salt spray attracted moisture from the air and created the goo running down the screens, onto the sills and even onto the wall below. Also, I had discovered that the metal bobbins for my sewing machine were getting rusty, and so were hand-sewing needles, if I left them out of their case even overnight. We should have known without being told that metal had a hard life on the island, as our refrigerator was pitted and pocked like a gallant old warrior.

We had trouble making paint stick to window sills on the ocean side of the house. Paint we meticulously put on walls and sills inside the house was bubbling and blistering after just two months.

There were all kinds of "old husbands' tales" about what painters could do to make paint adhere, and Ed tried more than one method with some, but not enough, success. The most interesting solution to the peeling paint problem was to pee in the paint—and mix it in. Something about making the paint more alkaline.

David Fleming, who had lived on the island in the winter for many years, had tried everything. He said he used to have the same problem on his pool deck, but through experimentation he had found that an oil-base paint mixed with clear stain 50/50 provided a sturdy finish. Three coats of this mixture, however, were required. He had decided to try another product he'd just heard about for his windowsills: "Reliance Surface Conditioner," which was a concrete primer. He would then paint on top of that.

The climate also was hard on metal coat hangers, which rusted within a few weeks. So we bought plastic ones to replace them. Rubber bands and elastic also fell prey to the elements. We saved rubber bands from an early death by keeping them in the refrigerator. And I also took anything with elastic back north with me over the summer. I learned this the hard way when a slip, left in a dresser drawer for six months, fell to my ankles while I was getting ready for church one Sunday morning. We had long lists of what we took back up and then back down. Without lists, we would have forgotten important things like underpants and slips.

Occasionally, I did something I never would in the States; I removed the relaxed elastic in a pair of shorts and replaced it with new. This was particularly true if I liked the shorts and wore them all the time. Since clothing wasn't easy to find on the island, especially in the right size, the only way out was a repair job, an SOS letter or phone call to a friend in the US or a rush trip to Puerto Rico.

Important pieces of equipment were always breaking down. William's freezer refused to work, so he and Ed moved the little portable one that came with our house down to his house. At about the same time, our front gate fell off because one of the hinges came loose from the post. This required a Herculean effort on Ed's part to prop it back up with the aid of 2 x 4s and some heavy wire—a temporary fix. We couldn't go without a gate even for a half hour because of all the loose animals in the neighborhood.

Sharon Jones, whose gate had been damaged in the hurricane, had hers re-hung, and we asked who did the repair. A Mr. Allen "up in the village," she said, "but he's hard to catch." Mr. Allen answered the phone when we called, agreed to come down to look at the gate, then showed up when he said he would, bringing tools, cement and a bracket he had fabricated. Within two hours, the repair was made. He even incised lines into the wet cement to make the patch look like the stones of the gate post. We were astounded.

Our windows were open unless it was storming, and we were in and out of the house a lot, so mosquitoes sometimes sneaked in. Just one or two, or so we thought. But eventually it seemed we had more than just a few. Ed said he thought he saw mosquitoes hovering around the front of the refrigerator, and we often found dead mosquitoes on our kitchen counters. With some sleuthing, we discovered that the culprit was the drip pan under the refrigerator. Health officials had been warning people to get rid of standing water on their property to forestall an epidemic of dengue fever, so this was a discovery of some importance. We henceforth made it a point to empty the drip pan more often.

There was a constant battle with termites. Albert Sullivan from White's Pest Control had told us there must be a nest somewhere close to our house, perhaps in the vacant land just up the hill. He believed that would explain why there were so many exploratory tunnels going up the wall behind our pool.

When we had returned that year after spending six months in Indiana, there was a snaking tan mark—as if a tunnel had been on the back door of our house near the kitchen but had been brushed off—maybe by the young man who cut our grass. Sullivan thought termites had been scouting our roof for a possible meal.

This activity in our absence was a bit creepy. I wondered what would happen if we didn't show up for two years and no one paid attention. It seemed certain that the termites would gain a foothold that might be hard to dislodge. We had to be vigilant all the time or task somebody else to be vigilant when we couldn't be.

After hacking at the undergrowth just over the pool wall, Ed did find one live termite nest, but it was up in a tree, not on the ground as he'd thought more likely. As a stop-gap measure, he soaked the nest with Malathion and called the pest control company to ask Sullivan for a special return visit.

Keeping termites away from our house was a constant battle. I told our pest control company, with which we had a contract, that we had the nasty critters in one of our palm trees and in the grapefruit tree behind the house. I had seen the trails snaking up from the ground and into the trees, but couldn't determine from where they had come.

Sullivan, who always did our spraying, searched around our property and found three large termite nests just over our fence in a large vacant area. He drove back to Plymouth that very day and returned with more equipment with which to do a 40-minute, heavy-duty spraying. Of course, there had to be a limit as to how far afield to go looking for nests. You couldn't spray the world in an effort to eliminate termites so they wouldn't bother your house. Over the fence in the vacant pasture behind our house seemed reasonable, when we considered that scout termites could build a tunnel from 50 feet away and into the doorjamb of a house in, literally, a few hours.

Our propane gas oven was losing heat because the gasket hung askew. This made us late eating sometimes when I misjudged the effect of the gasket on heat production. The "cooker" was an English model made by a company in Leamington Spa, Great Britain sometime in the 1960s. It had a small oven, and the broiler was a rudimentary flamethrower-like gizmo where I made toast in the morning. We didn't have a toaster. On a trip to England about a year later, we visited Leamington Spa and purchased a replacement gasket.

Home decoration proceeded slowly because not much was available on the island. If you wanted something, you either made it yourself or bought it when you were up north and brought it down the following winter. The light fixture over our dining room table was a case in point. It was metal of some unknown composition, and it was all rusty and dented as a result of Hurricane Hugo. It really needed to be thrown away. I had never seen such things in town. But, again, I could envision a nightmare if I tried to buy a chandelier back-up and brought it down.

So I decided to make a chandelier of macramé such as I'd seen at Nancy's house. I had never made anything of macramé, not even when it was popular in the 1960s, but felt sort of confident I could follow directions and turn out a product I wouldn't be ashamed of.

Nancy was glad to let me borrow the instruction leaflet, which included several designs, so I would know what kind of supplies I needed to buy in the US. Nancy had been successful finding the cord and a metal frame in Canada; I found the frame from a mail-order place in Maine and the cord in a hobby shop in Indiana when I went back to Indianapolis.

I made bedroom curtains, flimsy curtains I hoped would flutter in the breeze and make the room look cool and inviting. A situation, however, arose. On the Eastside of Montserrat, the breeze in December and January, and, it turned out, in half of February, blew with force so hard that the curtains, which were floor length, flapped horizontally. One night, Ed was sleeping unusually soundly and didn't realize one curtain had blown over and onto the bed. He rolled over on it and then rolled up in it and soon, confused in the dark, he muttered, "What happened here?"

After his cocoon experience, I reworked the curtains, cutting them short enough to end up, when hemmed, as deep valances. Friends from up north were astounded to watch this vestige of my dream curtains flapping like flags in the wind.

Situations with the water over time became a problem. After one choir practice, the water went off, and it was still off by the next morning. We didn't work in the yard that morning as we usually did. Getting sweaty was not a good thing to do when the water was off. The water was back on when we returned home from a short shopping trip into Plymouth, so we immediately took showers. It was a good thing, because, while I was making batches of guava jam and frozen yogurt that afternoon, the water went off again. Ed dipped a five-gallon bucket of water from the swimming pool so I could wash dishes and so we could flush the toilet.

The water had not been turned on by the next morning. But shortly after lunch, service was restored, sort of. There was just a trickle coming out of the tap, meaning we were not really in the clear. We took quick showers so that, hopefully, we would be somewhat clean the next time the water disappeared.

I never realized how much we took reliable water for granted until we didn't have it. I frankly didn't know what people without swimming pools were doing as we never knew when the tap would suddenly yield absolutely nothing. Nor did we ever know how long the outage would last.

One day, when we walked up the hill to get our mail, we noticed water spurting up in the middle of a field. Upon closer inspection, we realized someone had tethered a cow to a water pipe and in poking around the cow had ruptured it. Or at least that's what we thought had happened. Several cows were standing around looking stupid and nonplussed, as only cows can look. As it was nearly dark, we thought it unlikely the water company would come out right then to fix the leak, which probably would mean that our water supply would dwindle down and then disappear, to be off all night and into the next morning.

We kept a list of our water outages over the prior 10 days, and Ed wrote a letter to the editor of the newspaper, including the list. He also drove a copy of the letter and the list to Samuel Roach, who was the government representative for the East district of Montserrat and also the minister of public works. (We thought it would be a politic thing to do to give Roach a chance to see the letter before it appeared in the newspaper.)

While we were at his house, having orally briefed him about the water problem, he called the water authority and got no answer. He sympathized with our problem, but didn't make any promises. The water came back on, but sometime in the night, it went off again. We heard the pipes clanking at 5 a.m., signifying the water had been turned on again. But there was so much air in the pipes and the pressure was so low that our hot water heater, which worked only on demand, would not kick in. Thinking that the water might go off again at any moment, we quickly took cold showers.

Ed's letter had some effect. Beth Green Farrell, the manager of the water authority, called us on the phone and said she wanted to meet with us on the upcoming Monday at 10:30 a.m. "to talk about some of the problems you're having in Spanish Point."

Water from the skies also was unreliable during the winter months. When stored water became seriously depleted, Montserrat instituted water conservation measures. The directive was announced on Zed Jay Bee that pumps would be shut off on a large part of the island Monday, Tuesday, Friday and Saturday from 9 p.m. to 5 a.m. The other parts of the island would have their water shut off on the other days.

In addition, residents were asked not to water grass or their gardens or wash their cars from a hose. I suppose this also meant we were not supposed to top off swimming pools. We knew that drought conditions existed when the hibiscus dropped their leaves.

It was Ed's contention that the water-saving ploys instituted by the government would not work. When the water was turned back on after a shut-off period, householders had to run it a long time in order to get air out of the pipes and clear out the rust, Ed said in a letter to the *Montserrat News*, an upstart newspaper that was not in the pocket of the government.

All the water, of course, was metered, so you had to pay for it, even during a clearing-out-the-rust period. In addition, turning water off from 9 p.m. to 5 a.m. didn't cut consumption because most people were sleeping then. About 700 gallons per day, according to a neighbor who obsessively monitored such things, was spilling out into a watering trough and then onto the ground in lower Spanish Point.

We knew that we were becoming obsessed with water, or our lack thereof. On the morning news, we heard that in addition to the four nights with water off each week, the center of the island would have taps shut off every day from 9 a.m. to 3 p.m. Trucks would come around to supply people who needed water, the announcer said. Spanish Point was not included in the area where the new shut-offs would occur.

It seemed to us that the springs from which the island obtained its water were drying up, and no one knew why. Rumors and conspiracy theories abounded. William said he didn't think the island was really short of water at all. Instead, he thought the water authority was attempting, by shutting off the pipes, to save money on electricity. His theory, I guess, was as good as any other. When he was a boy, streams on the island rushed with water, William said, and at present they were dry beds with water in them only when it rained. Back then, though, I thought, there weren't as many people. Also those who did reside on the island did not have running water in their homes, so the demand was much less.

In the same extended conversation, sitting on our porch after dark, William said that, between 1956 and 1986, he was working in England, although he made seven trips back to Montserrat to visit his mother. He wryly commented that the woman "ought to be thinking about being with her Lord."

Many individuals kept animals, but not all of them very well. Billy, for example, had a brown cow, which we thought was a calf. But when it was the same size in a year, we decided it was just malnourished. Sometimes, Billy would stake his cow in the pasture across from our gate for a couple of days. As far as I know, he never checked on its well-being.

Ed and I didn't realize this right away, not until the cow started bawling and wouldn't stop. Then we began to realize it wasn't a baby missing its mother, so Ed filled a five-gallon paint bucket with water and carried it over. At first, the cow was too nervous to drink with him close by, but when he walked away, she lapped up half the bucket.

We hated to overstep our bounds, but thought we ought to say something to Billy. He said he'd been very busy and promised he would take care of the problem. That day, he did walk the cow up to the trough near the clinic for a drink of water. But we didn't see where he tethered her after that. In about three weeks, he brought the cow back to the vacant lot across the street from our house —and left her there for two days.

Even tied-up animals caused problems: more situations. A sheep gave birth right in front of our gate, in the spot where she had been tethered. The lamb struggled away from her and then couldn't find its way back. I heard the frantic bleating of the mother, who needed the lamb to nurse, and the piteous crying of the tiny lamb, who was hungry and couldn't find its mother. Ed tied the ewe, a skinny little thing with the afterbirth still hanging out of her rear end, closer to her baby.

William had two black calves, about half grown, which he tethered near his house. We called them "William's Misters." They weren't a problem until they reached maturity; then they became interested in the females of the species and bellowed all night if a flirtatious bovine lady tip-toed through the neighborhood.

After one such siege, William called to apologize. He said a loose cow in the area had them quite excited. He admitted he had considered moving the "misters" farther away from our house, but their level of excitement scared him off. They calmed down, and he did take them one by one to a spot where we could neither see nor hear them. As time went on, William became more frightened of the misters. He announced one day that he planned to sell the bulls to the butcher the following Monday. They had matured to the point they were fighting each other. "If they kill each other," he said, "I will have nothing." I asked him how much they weighed, and he said he was selling them by the animal and not by the pound, so he didn't know. William said he hadn't intended to sell them so soon, but he just couldn't handle them any more. Besides, he had heard about a "chap" in Salem, a town on the Northwest side, who was gored by his bull and ended up in the hospital.

As it turned out, William sold only one of his misters because he and the potential buyer of the second bull had not been able to agree on a price. One night shortly thereafter, we barely got any sleep because the remaining bull, tethered in the vacant lot across from our house, and the dogs of Denton O'Garro, a neighbor from up the hill in Spanish Point, barked and bellowed by turns. O'Garro raised pigs in his backyard and once we saw him butchering a cow along our unpaved road.

O'Garro maintained a shop in the open-air market downtown; it had been the established place to buy food before the supermarkets came into being. We sometimes wandered in just to see what was happening there. On one occasion, he was cutting up a pig on a scarred-up wooden table, its bloody snout dangling in a nearby sink. I wondered what a board of health in the US would say.

Perhaps it was because O'Garro was born on another Caribbean island that he didn't think he needed to abide by Montserrat's rules. Or perhaps he was just slovenly. One thing I know: He threw cabbages into his backyard from his pick-up truck, and as far as I could tell, he never cleaned up anything. Another thing I know: when the wind was right, we and William could smell his farming operation. William called the stench "unpleasant."

Butchering on your home premises was against the law, if you intended to sell the meat to the general public. All meat for public consumption was supposed to be butchered at the abattoir. My understanding, however, was that you could butcher at home for your own use, as William did, and there was no law against that.

Mostly old ladies were the vendors at the market. They uniformly wore what we would have, in the '40s, called "housedresses" and hats, often made of felt. Almost without exception, they kept bills and change in plastic bags tucked into pockets of colorful aprons. They weighed produce, tomatoes, lettuce, green beans, on rusty scales and kept records in little account books. This was definitely low-tech, so it was amusing to see a girl of about 10, probably a grandchild of one of the salesladies, playing a hand-held video game.

Another cow, not belonging to William, bellowed two days in a row and one whole night. And Ed, stretched to the limit, decided to take action. To our knowledge, no one had given the cow any water. It was tethered to a small tree, which Ed dug up, whereupon the cow took off, dragging the trunk behind. To be sure, the farmer would not like the cow bellowing outside HIS window at 2 a.m. Several Spanish Point residents told me they'd also cut animals loose that weren't watered or moved for days. They also cut loose animals tethered where they could poop on driveways or where they could eat plantings. It was very easy to become obsessed by the animal situation; then it became a problem. We tried not to obsess, unless a particular beast somehow found its way into our yard or kept us awake all night.

A helicopter was seen flying up and down the ghauts, and neighbors started talking. What could this mean? Ed and I figured the authorities were looking for pot plants. Somebody else thought an evil-doer, perhaps the pot grower, was hiding out in a ghaut to avoid detection. After a few days, we learned from someone who probably knew what she was talking about that the British navy had been commissioned to help the island get rid of derelict cars, which lined the roads in remote areas and were seen here and there even near Plymouth. Sometimes, young men pushed the cars into the ghauts just to get rid of them. On a 39 1/2 square mile island, there was no place to put trash of such size. Indeed, disposing of trash and garbage, big or little, was one of Montserrat's biggest "situations".

The intention was, we learned, to have the helicopter lift cars out of the remote resting places, whereupon anything toxic or usable would be removed. Then the helicopter would carry the cars one at a time just offshore near a place called Bransby Point where they would become part of an artificial reef. But there was an apparent problem: The cars were too heavy for the helicopter.

Despite the island's situations and true problems, living there could be idyllic—no worries and a beautiful environment. By February of each year, the water in our pool was warm enough we could swim our laps at 4:30 p.m. During December and January we had to swim no later than 2:30 p.m. or the water cooled too much as the sun sank ever lower. Contrary to what most people think, the tropics are not warm all year around. I personally didn't like to swim when the ambient temperature was only 75 degrees with a stiff wind blowing.

While we were in the pool one afternoon, a young villager of about 14 showed up at our back fence. To get there, he had to fight his way through the tall weeds, bushes and low trees that nicely screened our property from view. I was always a bit put off when somebody came to the fence which ran across the back of our property. As a rule, nobody did. Most residents, at least on the Eastside where there were a lot of loose animals, had fenced and gated yards, and the unwritten code required a visitor to call at the gate for permission to enter. That was true no matter who the visitor was.

To have somebody suddenly appear no more than 15 feet from where we were swimming seemed quite an intrusion—especially since we sometimes did that in the nude. We tried to be friendly to the boy. He said he had never swum in a pool before, and then he asked all sorts of leading questions, such as "How deep is the water?" At last he asked what he really wanted to know. "Could I have a swim?"

Ed told him that since one child nearly drowned in our pool (which was true), we had made it a rule that any child who swam there must have a parent with him or her to assume responsibility. "If your mother or father will come with you, then, yes, you can have a swim," Ed said.

With that, the boy said, "Thank you" and crawled back through the bushes and away from the fence. And that was the end of that.

Because we were relatively young, I suppose that was the reason, we didn't think about health care beyond being grateful for the clinic and the knowledge that there were doctors and a dentist on the island.

We knew that the hospital was able to handle routine ailments, but anything unusual and dire emergencies had to be taken care of elsewhere. We guessed that a heart attack or a stroke might be a couple of those dire emergencies. It would take an ambulance 30 minutes to reach Spanish Point from the hospital in Plymouth and another 30 minutes back. Our best bet, we thought, was to summon one of the small aircraft of Montserrat Air Service and charter it to take the patient to Antigua 27 miles away, where, supposedly, the medical care was more advanced. The closest US-related hospital of any size was in Puerto Rico, about 300 miles away.

We didn't think about any of these potential problems as long as we were living on the island. Fortunately, our health was good, save for my high blood pressure, which was controlled with drugs that I brought down with me from Indianapolis.

14
METAL WORK

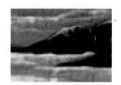

Renting a car worked well for us for a while, but as time went on, we decided owning one would be cheaper and would suit us better. Vic Henry said he had a car for sale; it was a Suzuki Swift, which was owned by the same couple who sold us the washing machine. They weren't coming back to the island, he said.

The car, which had a manual transmission, was perfect for us because, at that point, we had never driven anything else. One drawback was that it had been stored in the carport of the couple's house, which had been empty for at least two years.

Vic said the price was $5,200 US. The car had 8,000 miles on it, and although it bore a couple of crudely painted-over scratches down the side, courtesy of Hurricane Hugo, it seemed to be in good shape, on the outside at least. But on the inside, the carpet on the driver's side was ripped. Vic told us a rat climbed into the car because one of the windows was left partway open. The fact that the car had two new tires and a new brake job seemed more important than ripped carpeting.

Although we wanted to take possession as soon as we wrote a check, Vic's mechanic, Rondo, had not been able to clean the carburetor to his satisfaction. The little Suzuki, it turned out, had been stored with gas in the tank, and over the time it sat idle, the gas evaporated, leaving gunk. So we extended the rental car another couple of days until Rondo could work on our new purchase.

Because of the heat and humidity on Montserrat, something or other on the car needed to be repaired more often than we were used to. We'd had it maybe a month or six weeks when the tuning was so far off that our Suzuki died at inopportune moments. Rondo, whose real name was Rondell Cabey, took our car so he could work on the idle. He said he'd have it ready the next day, which I doubted, because Montserratians were not into details or schedules. But when the next day came, the car, miraculously, was ready. People hung onto cars until they literally fell apart, and we planned to be no exception. Rondo told us we needed new brakes and advised Ed to bring them down the next time we went back up and had access to auto parts stores.

That's the way it was when we went north. In addition to blood pressure medicine and underpants, we had to find the new muffler or brake pads we needed or the stove burner a neighbor needed. Our packing list was very long.

Rondo was an amazing guy. He worked as a Nissan mechanic in the daytime and then, at night, he repaired cars in his gas station near Harris'. He also designed and constructed ornamental grates for windows and doors. We thought it would be a good idea to have some of these grates because of our remote location, our previous break-ins and the fact that we were gone for six months each year.

He fabricated the grates from reinforcing rods, or rebar, which he bent into intricate patterns. We could see them, or pieces of them, propped against trees near his gas station/repair shop—a good advertisement.

Through Vic, we contracted with Rondo to build us grates for some windows and our back door. He said he would, but we waited several weeks for the grates to be finished because he was busy with his many pursuits. After Rondo fabricated our grates, he was supposed to paint them white. At last, he let us know that he was ready to deliver early the next morning. I waited around while Ed and some houseguests climbed Chance's Peak, then the tallest on the island. Although the 3,200 foot summit once had been accessible only by a tortuous path, the telephone company Cable and Wireless, which had an antenna there, built steps.

Rondo didn't show up. Several days later, while we were in Plymouth buying upholstery tacks and a comb for Ed, Rondo brought the grates and installed all but the two which would cover the glass in the back doors. For those, he had to get inside the house. Installing grates on the outside over the windows meant drilling holes in the concrete block, inserting the grates and then cementing them in. By the time we arrived home, Rondo was gone.

In mid-afternoon, he and his helper, a Rasta man named Izzy, came to finish the job. We had run into Izzy before, in the aftermath of having Rondo tune up the Suzuki shortly after we purchased it. When we returned to the gas station for a fill-up a few days later, Izzy asked Ed, "You fine a specky?" Ed couldn't figure out what he meant and had him repeat what he said. "Specky," Izzy said. "You fine a specky?" Then, Izzy said he thought he might have left the specky in our car.

Slowly, I came to realize that what he was saying was, "Spare Key." He had been working on our car, he said, and had the key to another car, belonging to another family, in his hand. He thought he might have put it into that bin in the passenger door where you could stash maps or sunglasses. We hadn't noticed the key, but sure enough, it was there.

Izzy and Rondo had last worked on our car several days before, and I wondered what the other family was doing for transportation before Izzy got around to asking us if we had found a spare key. Ever thereafter, our private habit was to refer to Izzy as "Specky."

Rondo wanted to be paid in full for the grates, but we weren't ready to close the deal quite yet. One of them was installed crookedly while we were in town, and the paint job on all was terrible—thick in some places and almost nonexistent in others. Although the grates were beautifully made and ingeniously designed, we wanted the job completed to our satisfaction before we paid Rondo his EC $3,200, which was a little over $1,000 US.

This interpersonal relationship was all quite sticky because we made the initial request for the grates through Vic Henry. This had been our mutual decision as the best way to handle the project because Henry was the overseer of our house when we were up north. So technically Henry should write the check to Rondo, and we should reimburse Henry.

So it was Henry that told Rondo the job was not done to the Elrods' satisfaction. The next day, Rondo roared up to our house in his truck, ranting and raving about not getting his check. He kept saying, "You don't trust me. You don't trust me." And Ed told him quietly and patiently—several times—that when he straightened the crooked grate, he would get his money. We would repair the paint job ourselves, we told him. Ed and I had privately talked a lot about our compromise. We concluded he was slow in building the grates, but needed the money, so when he finally had them constructed, he rushed the painting, brushing on some coats before the one underneath was dry. Or he put on a coat of paint only to have it rained on, then put on successive coats over dampness. Rondo straightened the crooked grate, and Vic Henry paid him. In the weeks that followed, we continued to patronize Rondo's gas station and never made mention again of the problem with the grates. We had no other choice but to forgive because there was only one gas station/repair shop on our side of the island. If the car needed fixing, he or Specky were the ones to make the repairs.

Increasingly Rondo was away from the station because he had been hired to repair big machinery at "the crusher," the local name for the quarry operation that had begun just up the mountain from the village of Farms. He hired a young woman to take care of pumping gas at the station.

One day when we needed gas we found her sitting on a stool watching the inauguration of Bill Clinton broadcast live on Antigua TV. I discovered later that Guadeloupe radio was airing the whole ceremony in English and translating it into French. I wondered whether in the States we would carry live the entire inauguration of the German chancellor or the British prime minister. It was awesome to consider in what high esteem some foreign countries held, and do hold, the United States.

The Suzuki key was long and had a narrow "waist," which we didn't realize the import of until it broke off in the gas tank lock. So we drove into Plymouth the next day to have a copy made.

Our first stop was Emerald Building and Supply, which we thought would be a likely place to have a key made. We were told, however, that "Manuel," the man who operated the cutting machine, was gone to "the East," the very part of the island we had just left. Ed thought he had seen a key-cutting machine at the Toyota dealership down in Plymouth, so we drove there. The guy behind the counter affirmed the existence of a key-cutting machine but said they didn't carry the blanks for it. He said Ed could buy those at Osborne's, which was next door to Emerald, where we had just been. "That's why I love this place," Ed said to me, relating what had happened.

So we drove back up the hill, purchased the blank from Osborne's, which didn't have a key cutting machine, and returned to Toyota, where the man made us a duplicate key. It worked. About a month later, Ed broke off the other original Suzuki key, not the duplicate we had just bought. This meant we would have to get a duplicate made from a duplicate, a dicey proposition.

He first stopped at Osborne's to buy a blank and then to the Toyota dealership, which had the key cutting machine. The first attempt didn't work, either in the door or the ignition, so Ed took the new key back to the guy who made it and complained. The Toyota counterman lined up the new key with the old one, which worked, and took off a little bit here and a little bit there. This time, the key didn't work the first time Ed tried it in the ignition, or the second time, but on the third try, the motor turned over. This did not seem dependable enough, however, so Ed took the key back yet another time for fine-tuning.

The result was worse; it didn't work at all. The situation seemed to be a real problem, at least in my eyes. Ed decided the only thing to do was to return to Osborne's for another key blank and start over. The woman behind the counter at Osborne's, understanding Ed's frustration, asked him what had gone wrong and, then, what kind of a car we had. When Ed said it was a Suzuki, she said, "Well, in that case, since the car was originally bought here because Osborne's is the only Suzuki dealer on the island, we would have a record of the key number." All we needed to do, she said, was let her order another key from Suzuki in Barbados. This key would definitely work, as it would be an original, not a copy of a copy. The cost would be only EC $5 more than what we had already spent on the key blank and cutting.

For a week, until the new key came from Barbados, we would have to be very, very careful.

I finally got up my courage after several nightmares over several months and drove the car the six miles into Plymouth. It did not add to my confidence when we learned that a couple of teen-agers had driven their car over the side into one of the ghauts near our house. Fortunately, they weren't hurt, but they weren't rescued right away either. A passer-by happened to see the car and helped the occupants crawl out and up the steep bank. It was said around the island that the teens were high on ganja, or "weed." As we were passing by a few days after the accident, a truck with a winch was hauling the car out of the ghaut.

My maiden trip to town came off without incident, but I was grateful it wasn't possible to drive much over 25 MPH. Ed said there was only one place on the island where he might be able to go 40, and that was the long, straight and level stretch of perhaps two miles near the village of Cork Hill on the Westside side of the island.

Although I had put off driving, I knew this was not smart. I am not the sort of woman who likes to be dependent upon someone else for something as basic as transportation and was frankly surprised at myself for dragging my feet so long. Suppose Ed got get sick; I would have to drive. The longer I put it off, the less likely I might be to ever get behind the wheel on the island, although I drove everywhere up north.

But then I thought of our neighbor Mildred, who spent the winter on the island and didn't drive. She was perfectly content, she said, to ride the bus, but only the bus on which the riders were not allowed to swear.

Sometimes, it was difficult to relax and enjoy our lives, especially when our mechanical gadgets, such as our car and the lawn mower, weren't functioning well. Rondo hadn't had the time to repair our lawn mower, although Vic took it to him two weeks earlier. So on a trip into town we stopped at Rondo's service station to check on his progress, if any. He promised to work on the mower that very day, and we agreed to return in the late afternoon to pick it up.

Having access to the mower was becoming more important by the day because the grass in our yard was a foot tall. But when we returned later that afternoon, Rondo looked sorrowful when he said, "There's a problem with your mower." This we knew. When pressed as to what he meant, he said, "Your mower is in the afternoon of its life." In short, he didn't think it might be fix-able, or, at least, worth fixing. Although we didn't want to spend the money, we decided we had to buy a new one.

The next morning early we headed for town to look for a simple lawnmower. We walked around to the various hardware stores to see what they had for sale, if anything, and discovered that the only store displaying a lawnmower of any kind was Grimes.' Their mower was made in Tennessee and carried an EC $711 price tag, or about $260 US.

At the time, our first thought was that this was an outrageous price. What could we do? The mower was imported, after all. We couldn't take the lawnmower home that day. The one on display wasn't available for purchase, the sales clerk said, and all the rest in stock needed to be put together. So we would have to come back the next day to take delivery.

There was always something on the car that needed repairing, it seemed. It wasn't long before our Suzuki began to die at inopportune moments, so Ed made an appointment with Rondo. When we showed up at his station, however, the woman who worked there said he had gone to the crusher. If the equipment at the quarry broke down, he had made an arrangement to drop everything and attempt to fix whatever was wrong. So Ed drove back home and inadvertently left the headlights on. He didn't discover this until just before dinner. By then the car didn't just die sometimes; it was totally dead.

He rolled the car down the hill in an effort to make the motor turn over. It wouldn't. He called our neighbor, Nancy, to ask for the use of her jumper cables. She wasn't home. Neither were the Henrys. There was no AAA on the island, so no help there. He then called Helen's house and hit the jackpot. Everyone he had phoned earlier was at her house playing bridge. Nancy agreed that, when the game was over, she would drive over with her jumper cables. It was after 10 p.m. when she showed up, and Ed was quickly able to get our car going again.

(You soon learned who had which tools. Vic had the sledgehammer. The Stewarts had jumper cables and a chain saw. We had purchased a long-handled "lopper" for pruning tall trees. Maybe that would become our claim to fame in the neighborhood.)

The next year, the brakes were squeaking badly, a sure sign that Rondo needed to get busy replacing them. Luckily, Ed had sensed an impending problem with brakes, so he'd bought new ones while we were up north and brought them down in his suitcase. But the brakes he was sold in Indianapolis were the wrong size and configuration for our model of Suzuki. Rondo called Osborne's, the Suzuki dealership in Plymouth, to see if it had the proper brakes in stock. The person who answered the phone said he thought so. Rondo said he would try to exchange the brakes Ed brought down for the right ones on the following Monday.

Rondo didn't have time to check right then, so we drove into town to see if we could trade the brakes ourselves. Osborne's didn't have the proper brakes, even though it was a Suzuki dealership. But it did have a muffler, which we also needed. The muffler had been removed from a Jeep, and the service rep said he thought it would fit our car. Ed said he wanted Rondo to have a look at it before he paid what he thought was an outrageous price. The Toyota dealership and auto parts store next to Ram's supermarket didn't have the brakes or the proper muffler, but did have tires. You had to buy tires just about every two years because of the heat and humidity. (Once, I was weeding in the front yard next to the car when a tire went "bang" and blew out.)

We tried the Texaco station near the jail downtown and discovered that they had the brakes we needed and wanted only $35 US for them. We knew they were the right size and configuration because Ed earlier asked Rondo to take one of our brakes off and draw around it. Luckily, we ran into Rondo, also shopping in town, and he said he would put on the new brakes Saturday morning. That was fortunate. I had begun having nightmares about driving over a cliff because of brake failure.

We checked out a new grocery, which a neighbor said "is going to give Ram's a run for its money." There, we bought imported carrots, meaning they were more than three inches long and not bent and warty like the local ones. At Papa's supermarket, we bought frozen yogurt and fresh spinach. When Saturday came, we drove to Rondo's service station carrying the brakes we'd bought. The broken down tractor/trailer he was using as a parts department was hanging wide open, but neither Rondo nor Izzy was anywhere around. Izzy's mutt, Ali, came walking slowly up to us, however, wagging her tail.

Desperate by this time to have the new brakes put on, we decided to wait a few minutes to see if the two mechanics would show up. So we settled in to read, I, on the guts of an old car seat with Ali on the ground at my feet. In about 20 minutes, Rondo drove up in a car, which, in the States, would have been totaled. In no time, Rondo finished replacing the worn-out brakes. He didn't want to be paid until the following week, he said, because he hoped to find a muffler for us by then. The Jeep muffler we had located wouldn't fit, Rondo said. There was some urgency to having the new muffler put on, as the old one made us sound like a motorboat. Before he exchanged the brakes, we were a motorboat with a squeal. Luckily, the police on Montserrat never arrested anyone for noise pollution.

Some days later, Rondo yelled at us as we drove by on the way into town and said he would call ahead to Osborne's and that we should go there and pick up our new muffler. But he had been called to the crusher, which meant he wouldn't have time to work on our car that day. Days went by, and our car sounded worse by the minute. Ed had been leaning on Rondo, leaving messages on his answering machine, a rarity for the island in 1995. When we stopped by on our way into town, Rondo could be seen looking up a phone number, no doubt that of Tim Evans, a purveyor of car parts, where Rondo had told us at one point he'd found a muffler that would probably fit our car.

We made an appointment with Rondo for the next day. We showed up at the appointed hour, 8:30 a.m., having purchased the muffler from Tim Evans the previous afternoon. But Izzy said Rondo wasn't there as he had to tow a car. With that, Izzy climbed into an ancient red station wagon, saying he would be back in a "short while." About the same time, it began to rain.

Since we had such a hard time even acquiring the muffler, we decided to sit and wait for Rondo to return. He had a stack of very old magazines, and I settled in to read. An hour later, Rondo and Izzy drove up. "Sorry about that," Rondo said. Ed grunted. After that, Rondo was quite grumpy, but he set to work, along with Izzy. Archie Dubin, a neighbor in Spanish Point, drove up a few minutes later and told Rondo he needed to have his muffler adjusted. Rondo had just replaced Archie's and for the same reason we also needed a replacement: the yearly inspection.

Because it would be another hour until our car was repaired, Archie decided not to wait, and Ed asked him to take me home. On the way, Archie told me he'd recently had his car inspected with the new muffler lying in the backseat. He told the inspector he was intending to have it installed, so the inspector never even asked him to turn the engine on. He just tested the lights. Supposedly, the inspection process was going to be easier because we no longer had to go to two places for different aspects of the test. According to the announcer on the radio, the inspection would be "one stop shopping." But five people were involved in the process, which included voluminous paperwork, so we didn't get finished in a hurry. Unlike the year before, only the lights and turn signals, not the brakes, were checked out. I'm not sure the inspectors noticed we had a new muffler.

Unfortunately, the new muffler clanked against the chassis. But when Ed, in a couple of weeks, went up to the gas station to find out when Rondo could look it over and eliminate the noise, the woman who worked there said he had been sick for 10 days and not at work.

Well, everybody has a right to be sick.

15
POSTAL SERVICE

On most trips to Plymouth to visit the hardware store or the grocery, we also went to the open-air post office, which was the center of life on the island. Upcoming events were advertised on handbills taped to the aqua-colored walls, and anyone with anything to sell could put up a notice.

Across from the clerk's windows, which were shuttered when the post office was closed, a paper cup full of water for moistening stamps sat on a counter. There was no wastebasket, so there was no place to put the paper edges from sheets of stamps. A tiny mentally handicapped man with a broom cleaned up the trash outside the post office. He was a fixture there, a source of questions about all sorts of issues raised in any society, but answered differently in all of them. For whatever reason, there were many mentally handicapped people on the island, and you couldn't miss them. Unlike in some societies, they weren't hidden away.

The little man, whose name I never learned, had a rather odd work habit. After he swept up a pile of trash, he pushed it through holes in the decorative concrete block which formed a wall between the post office and the lawn outside. Nobody in the post office told him how to do his job, apparently, and neither did the customers. Out of sight; out of mind.

He had another habit a bit more worrisome—begging for money, especially from white people and more especially from tourists. As soon as you walked up the steps to the open-air hallway where the stamp windows were, he crept up beside you and put his small, soft hand close to your body, never speaking, never touching you, only imploring you with his baleful eyes. You could chase him away with a firm "no," but walk away from the stamp window and he was there at your side again, as if he forgot his earlier encounter. Ed would sometimes give him a small coin, but not always. Sometimes, he would just shake the little man's hand and wish him well.

Mildred, who was black, lived in Toronto and stayed on Montserrat only in winter, took the beggar to task one day, telling him he was a disgrace, that he shouldn't be taking advantage of people that way and that she never wanted to see him there begging again. This harangue had no effect. He apparently had some sort of agreement with postal employees because he gave any money he got from begging to one of them for safekeeping, a pocketful at a time. I was told he didn't earn a salary, so begging was his only income. I also heard via the grapevine that he spent most of what he earned on alcohol. I was never aware that he came to work drunk.

Mail and how we received it—or didn't—added some spice and some consternation to life on Montserrat. Mrs. Myers, the postmistress in our area, was a retired school teacher of the "old school." Her little house had no glass in the windows, which were closed at night with wooden shutters. There were no screens. When on the job, she wore dresses from perhaps the 1950s and the top of a nylon stocking knotted and pulled onto her head. In the late afternoon, people from as far away as the village of Farms, which was perhaps two or three miles from her house, would walk slowly over and form a queue outside her special window. She sat on a stool just inside the window to dispense the precious letters and also the bills. It was dark inside the house, so I was never able to see where she kept the mail. I fantasized that it was fastened with rubber bands to keep the villages separate.

One morning while we were working in the yard, Mrs. Myers phoned to say we had a package downtown at the post office and that we should pick up the receipt from her before we drove over to Plymouth to claim it. We imagined that it was probably a museum poster of a snow scene that a friend had given us while we were up north and that we had sent to ourselves before our recent trip down to spend the winter. We couldn't imagine what was the big rush. By the time we took showers, put on clean clothes and picked up the receipt, it was 10 a.m. We didn't realize that our timing mattered, so we drove across the mountains to Plymouth right away. However, we stopped at one of the drugstores before appearing at the post office. By then it was 11:30 a.m. The woman behind the counter said we were too late and that we should come back tomorrow at 9 a.m. Too late for what?

Too late to catch one of the customs officials, who had to look at the contents of the package and come up with a fee, it turned out.

We decided to do more shopping since we were in town already. One did not drive into Plymouth over those twisty roads without planning ahead, and we carried the "to buy" list with us. Many businesses closed at noon for lunch and re-opened at 1 p.m. or sometimes 1:30, and some closed on Wednesday afternoons. Some closed also on Saturday afternoons. The businesses that closed Wednesday p.m. weren't necessarily the same ones that closed Saturday p.m. Grimes' Wayside Store was open Wednesday all day but closed early Friday afternoon for the Seventh-day Adventist Sabbath and was closed all day Saturday. Almost nothing was open on Sunday. There was a push afoot to talk businesses into staying open during lunch and on Wednesday afternoons so tourists and office workers could shop then, but, mostly, storekeepers were not persuaded.

As we were told to do, we returned to the post office at 9 a.m. the next day to retrieve our package from customs. This time, the woman said the customs agent was busy distributing the mail and wasn't available to release our package to us. She was quite surly, we thought, particularly when she asked us to stand a few feet from the parcel window.

While we were waiting, Ed asked me to go to the Royal Bank of Canada to pick up a fax that had been sent to us from a friend in Indianapolis. The arrangement was that this friend would pick up our mail, deposit any insurance commission checks to our checking account and fax us a weekly report showing the bills we owed. We had been warned not to try to have mail gathered up and sent to Montserrat from the States, as mail took a long time reaching the island and was sometimes missent.

It wouldn't do to have our "bock-up" light or water bill sent to Calcutta, India, as later happened to a Christmas card sent to us from Indiana—bearing the correct postage and the correct address. By mistake, pieces of mail also went to Antigua, Jamaica, St. Maarten in the Netherland Antilles, Barbados, Tortola, Germany and Indonesia. One letter was postmarked in Indianapolis on February 12 and reached us on April 12. Routinely, mail from the States took two weeks to reach us.

If we didn't receive the fax at the agreed-to time, I panicked. The monthly money situation had become quite tight because of an unexpected repair on the Indiana car and a 60 percent increase in our already large insurance premium for the Montserrat house. The company said the increase was necessary because of all the natural disasters in the Caribbean and in Central America, earthquakes in Guatemala and Hurricane Hugo.

After I had waited in line a few minutes at the bank, Ed appeared with a fat mailing tube, somewhat the worse for wear, under his arm. It was indeed the poster of a snow scene, which we intended to have framed on the island so we could hang it in our bedroom.

Ed said the tube had been broken almost in two somewhere in transit, and the poster was badly wrinkled, but not torn. He said the woman at the post office had run him through a humiliating routine of carrying the box a few feet, placing it on a spot she indicated on the table, then having him move it again because she wasn't satisfied with precisely where he set it down. Only then could the customs official look at the contents. He charged Ed $5 US for what was essentially a damaged poster, perhaps too damaged to be salvaged.

Some of the surplus textbooks that a friend in Indianapolis found were shipped directly to the Seventh-day Adventist School, Mrs. Grimes' daughter told us. One box had arrived, and the other boxes were at the post office awaiting pick-up. Luckily, the friend who found the books and her husband were visiting us at that exact time, and we were all invited to the school so we could see where the treasure would be used and to meet the children. Mrs. Grimes' daughter said she would call us later to give us a time. That afternoon, she called to say we should be at the school at 10 a.m. the next day.

The principal, Letitia Grimes, met us at the door of the Seventh-day Adventist school, a long, low, concrete-block building that looked as if it had been under construction a long time. Indeed, the building was being put together bit by bit on weekends and days off by parents of the pupils, she told us. Being a parochial school, it received no money from the government and had to rely on donations and tuition.

The children, all dressed in shades of blue, were quietly doing their lessons when we arrived. When we entered an area—mostly the students were in one big room, with the classes separated by screens—all the pupils and their teacher stood up, respectfully. A goal of the school, Mrs. Grimes said, was to create servants who would use their talents to make their communities better.

One class, well-scrubbed and well-behaved, sang us a song about praising God, being cheerful and doing good. But the school was, apparently, not mainly about big smiles and a happy heart. Ed noted that the math lessons on the blackboards looked quite complicated for the grade level in which they were being taught.

When we received no mail, and particularly on days when the weather was rainy, and the Antigua TV's evening news had only five minutes of international news, we felt somewhat cut off from the outside world. The Antigua international news reports came at the end of the local news, weather and sports. We thought it funny that dominoes was included as a sport.

The only way we could remedy our lack of news was by subscribing to cable TV, which we didn't want to do. We discovered our best chance to get US news was from the BBC or Voice of America on the radio.

Montserrat had, at the time, one newspaper, a weekly, which contained news of the island, mostly, with a few stories about happenings elsewhere in the Caribbean. We could buy a Caribbean weekly, in addition, and once in a while, *Time* and *Newsweek* magazines. When friends about to come to the island for a visit asked what we'd like from the States, we didn't even have to think. One couple brought us *The Indianapolis Star* from the day they left home as well as a *Boston Globe* they'd picked up in the airport. I had to force myself to play hostess to them when what I really wanted to do was settle into a quiet corner with the newspapers.

A few days later, when I happened to be at the Montserrat Golf Club, I spied a copy of *The New York Times* lying on a table and pounced on it like a vulture on road-kill. I didn't care that it was two months old.

Going to get the mail was the highlight of many people's days, even if the "gift" of the day was only a bill. It was there, standing in line, that you could learn lessons in patience and compassion. Medford was often sitting alone on Mrs. Myers' porch while we were finding our place in line. One day, I noticed that he had a big bandage on his head. "Did you fall down?" I asked.

"No, Aunty Carol," he said. "I've been stung by a Jack Spaniard. It raised a big bump, and there is some pus." From the end of the school day until his mother returned home from her job, Medford waited on Mrs. Myers' porch, sitting patiently, with no toys to play with, no books to read, no nothing—his only stimulation provided by the villagers stopping by to pick up their mail and talk to him. The same trait could be seen in other children, yet they seemed happy as well as contented.

16
FRIENDS AND NEIGHBORS

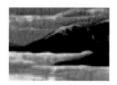

Some thought the local Rastas used "weed" as part of their religious practices, but maybe they didn't. Who knew? When
we first visited the island, in the spring of 1992, we didn't see many
Rastas, or people we thought were Rastas because of their dreadlocks.
As time went on, it was much more common to see young men with
dreads, often wearing enormous tams crocheted or knitted of gold,
green, red and black.

Our neighbor, Carlton, was not a Rasta man, but maybe had been
a wannabe in the past. In the present, he was a mental patient, a status thought by some to have been caused by heavy drug use. I'd guess
he was in his 30s when we knew him, a sad and sometimes humorous
man who could have contributed to the island community had he
made better choices when he was a teen-ager. Margaret said he once
had a good job, had been a member of the Bethel Methodist Church
and even had sung in the choir.

It was at choir practice where I heard that Carlton was "off his
meds." When I said something to Margaret about Carlton, she said
I should be careful what I said because his sisters—who might or
might not share the same last name, I found out—still were members
of the church. In fact, two sang in the choir.

Carlton had a "Hugo House," given him by the government, but
he preferred to sleep al fresco in the wreck of a house down by the
ocean in Spanish Point. Lucy Evans, who ran the Meals on Wheels
program, said he could be stabilized by getting a shot at the clinic,
but sometimes he refused to go. He used to be friendly with the nurse
who was stationed there, and she could usually talk him into taking
his needed medication. But, Lucy said, she married an American and

moved to the United States. And Carlton turned uncooperative. He wasn't cooperative with his family either. In fact, his only communication with them was cursing. He wasn't violent, however. If he behaved badly, Lucy said, the police would pick him up and take him either to prison or the hospital. He would always go quietly.

One day, we saw Carlton sitting on the ground across the street from the clinic, one of his favorite spots to hang out. As usual, he was clutching a briefcase, but this day he also had a manila envelope and a backpack. He was swearing loudly, mostly about money and the banks and how he had been screwed out of money. (There may have been an element of truth in what he said.)

We mentioned Carlton to the postmistress, Edith Myers, when we walked up to get our mail. She said she had no sympathy for him. "He got what he bought," she said. I took this to mean, as we had heard rumored, that he had fried his own brains. The neighbors looked out for Carlton, and this beneficence toward the not-so-normal was common on the island. One family gave him cigarettes and cans of tuna fish. We gave him coconuts and an occasional can of sardines. And others fed him leftover casseroles. None of it amounted to a lot, but it helped supplement whatever meager disability allowance he received from the government.

Sometimes, he was forthright about what he required, like the day he called at our gate to ask if we had any "dry nuts." That meant coconuts which had turned brown on the outside and in which you could hear the milk sloshing around. "Do you have a cutlass?" Ed wanted to know.

"Yes, mon," he said, pointing to his cutlass, which he had laid on the ground. In a little while, we could hear chopping, chopping, chopping coming from just outside our gate, but out of sight. When this went on for some time, Ed called out, "Are you still working on that same nut?"

"No, no," Carlton said. "It's another one. It was much too close to the fence." This meant that he had reached into our neighbor's yard and pulled a ripe coconut off the tree there. I worried about Carlton's teeth because of his strange diet. Even at his young age, he already had several teeth missing.

Most people, we included, talked to Carlton as if he were just plain folks, although you never knew what he was going to say. Ed asked him how he was one day, and Carlton answered, "Normal, thank you." Usually, he was found close to home: somewhere between Tuitt's and his Hugo House and the hurricane-wrecked house he preferred near the ocean. But, occasionally, he showed up in town. After we attended a story-telling contest in Plymouth, we found him standing on the sidewalk near the Shamrock Cinema, the venue for the contest. We asked if he wanted a ride home. He said he did. On the way back to the Eastside of the island, he talked on and on about an explosion in San Fernando New Jersey Chicago. There had been a pipeline explosion in New Jersey the week before; maybe that was what he meant. A few days previous, we had seen him leading a donkey he said was his. Later, he passed by our gate again and asked Ed if he'd seen his "pony." When we inquired about the welfare of the pony some time later, he said he thought a Rasta man in Long Ground had it.

With Carlton, you never knew what to expect. On our way up to Mrs. Myers' late one afternoon, we saw him wearing an almost-clean pair of black pants, sunglasses, an almost-clean turquoise T-shirt, his necklace of shells and black dress shoes without socks. We asked if he were going to pick up his mail, and he said no because he was going to a party. We inquired how his foot was because he had been limping. Hard shoes hurt his feet, Carlton said, looking down at the dress shoes. If Ed didn't want the running shoes he was wearing, Carlton said he would be glad to have them. He said he wore a size 12, but if Ed wore only an 11, or if he should wear a 13, whatever, any of them would work out just fine.

I had seen a family of Rastafarian children in our area and asked Lucy about them. Or at least I thought they were Rastas because of their dreadlocks, uncommon on the island's children. She said their step-mother was making them go to public school, although when their father had full custody, he didn't want them going to school at all. Lucy said there was a "commune" of Rastafarians living "up the mountain" above Tuitt's Village. "They grow weed up there," she said, adding that the little boys used to run around in loincloths and nothing else. A few days before, we had heard a rumor that the father put weed in the children's food. I didn't think I believed that.

The Rastafarians we knew, whether real practitioners or not, were gentle, friendly people. One of these was Brandon Timmons, a young man who lived in a little Hugo House perched at the edge of a steep ghaut. Brandon, who had his dreadlocks tucked up into the typical hand-knit hat, was listening to music as he trudged barefoot up the hill toward his home when we spotted him along the main road. We offered to take him the rest of the way home, and he climbed willingly into our car. He had been up in Long Ground, he said, "planting vines." We asked him if he meant pumpkins, and he said, "No, sweet potatoes."

He and another man had a plot in the hills near Long Ground because the rain was more reliable there, he said. Most of the farmers we knew on the island seemed to hedge their business by having more than one plot of land because of the difference in rainfall from one section of the island to the next. This meant walking long distances to hoe or weed and then home again, often carrying garden tools. We tried to help out by offering rides to farmers as often as possible.

Although 99.9 percent of the Montserratians on the island were good people, there were some, as in any society, who were not. We learned from Zed Jay Bee radio and from hearing people talk that a 43-year-old man had slashed two people to death with a cutlass and severely wounded his own grandmother. This rampage had occurred in the north of the island, about five miles away from our little villages. Members of our church said the man, who was well known to the people in his village, was on the loose for several hours, but was apprehended later the same night in, of all places, a ghaut near Katy's house.

The dead were two women—one 75 and one 89 years old. Both suffered severe head wounds from the cutlass blows. An 18-year-old girl survived the attack, but was injured. The Zed Jay Bee radio account didn't totally square with what I heard at choir practice, but I figured somewhere between the two accounts was probably truth. The radio account said he was 5´5˝, stocky, with a beard and a balding head. A lot of women, especially older women, were resting more easily after the alleged perpetrator was caught.

We were glued to the radio as more and more details of the bloody crimes emerged. The chief of police, who had a voice like Sean Connery, announced the arrest, but didn't talk about motives or any definitive identification. The deputy chief minister, attorney Erol Blake, made a little statement on the radio, saying that what happened was in no way the norm for Montserrat, which was known around the world for being peaceful, hospitable and friendly. He appealed to people to pray for the families of the victims and to care for each other. This was Montserrat's version of damage control.

In the meantime, talk of the crimes continued. Neighborhood dinner parties were always good places to learn the latest gossip. At Helen's one evening, we learned that the murderer's victims included a former teacher, now elderly, and the perpetrator's grandmother. Two days before the murders, so the story went, he had raped a 90-year-old amputee woman, and he might have also raped one of the women he killed. The so-called "facts" were, we thought, becoming embellished to the point that what was real was rapidly becoming obscured.

Then, the next day, while working at the French ceramic studio, Cissie and Nicole, both of whom lived in the area where the murders took place and were acquainted with all the victims, filled in more details. Their information was probably more correct than what we had received at the all-white neighborhood dinner in Spanish Point, or so we hoped.

They said the perpetrator's name was "Bad-boy Jinks," a name he'd picked up in childhood, and that he came to Montserrat after he got into trouble on Antigua for raping his mother. Apparently, according to Cissie and Nicole, on Montserrat he had tried to rape a 90-year-old woman who could barely walk, thus corroborating, at least partially, the story we heard in Spanish Point.

We learned from another Montserratian that Jinks escaped to the Southeast side of the island near Harris' village because there was a manhunt by citizen vigilantes in the village where the crimes occurred. If they had caught him, he would have been torn apart "limb from limb," our source said.

17
CELEBRATIONS

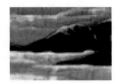

At Christmas, Montserratians who had moved to other countries to work returned to visit their parents and siblings. They arrived on charter airplanes as well as the regularly scheduled LIAT planes. Pilgrimages doubled the population of the island. We'd been told that many more former Montserratians lived in foreign countries—principally England, Canada and the United States—than lived on the island.

To please them, Montserratians still living on the island planned parties, sporting events, parades and contests. The women also did a lot of cooking and baking. On a Sunday morning just before Christmas, Sharon phoned to ask if her son Medford could sit with us in church because her sister, Angie, who was his usual seatmate, would not be attending the service. She had to do her holiday baking, Sharon said.

There were many visitors at that service, mostly from England. Two were godparents for two infants who were baptized. Quentin Plum, the Methodist minister, was a polished preacher, with tremendous stage presence despite his young age. On this occasion, he wore a long, white robe with a royal blue stole emblazoned with candles. Overhearing conversations after church, I understood that as time went by, the women of the church had come to love him to death. When he caught a cold, he was the recipient of enough soup to float the manse.

And I thought the United States went all out for Christmas. In many ways, the Monterratian celebration eclipsed it. To initiate the season, an all-island carol sing took place at the War Memorial in downtown Plymouth, and we decided to attend. Driving into town we picked up Katy Connor, who was waiting for a ride. I hardly recognized her: she was wearing a dress-up dress, a white hat and a black wig. Many of the older black women wore braids for everyday and wigs when they dressed up. Until I was used to this, I sometimes had a hard time figuring out who people were, especially in different settings.

The narrow road into town was crowded with cars and with people wanting rides. Without the white-gloved policemen directing traffic in Plymouth, it would have been difficult to pass through and find a place to park.

A sound system had been set up—with the ubiquitous huge speakers—and the singing was being broadcast live on Zed Jay Bee. The only problem was that the sing was held next to the War Memorial, where the clock registered each quarter hour. The singing groups had quite a lot of competition.

Emcee for the occasion was a large woman with a booming voice. Her hair was blowing in the warm breeze, and she kept an enormous purse tightly clasped to her body. Unfortunately, I believe, for us, the program started off with long-winded speeches by the chairman of the festival and a representative of the ministry of education. I say "only for us," because, for Montserratians, the carol singing was an excuse to be together and to chit-chat, no matter who was orating.

It seemed that every Montserratian we knew was there and hordes we didn't know, maybe 3,000 of them in all, huddled close to one another near the War Memorial, talking some and singing some. The audience ranged in age from babes in arms to old people. Expats were in short supply, but there were a few in the audience and a few in the singing groups.

A Christmas festival near the end of our stay on Montserrat was extra special because a Montserratian businessman with an unusually generous heart volunteered to purchase outdoor lights for downtown Plymouth. And MONLEC offered to put them up. About 1,500 people came downtown for the lighting ceremony. Unfortunately, the pre-lighting speeches went on for quite a while, so we needn't have hurried in getting there. Those who assembled for the lighting waited patiently, as Montserratians always did, for the speeches to end.

When the switch was thrown, only about half of the lights on the 1 1/2 miles of strings went on. No one uttered a cry of derision, and nobody prayed, at least audibly. There was not a sound. Soon, a MONLEC truck drove past the crowd and disappeared. In a couple of minutes, the lights came on. Then, the people cheered.

On the night before Christmas, it was the custom for Montserratians to do their shopping for gifts. All the stores were open, some until midnight, and there were tables along the sidewalk where volunteers wrapped gifts. Literally thousands of people went downtown to Plymouth, shopping and hanging out and listening to loud Soca music, which blared from giant loudspeakers.

Ed thought he would use the occasion to find a plastic watchband to replace a leather one that had broken, victim of sweat and heat. No one had any. Several shopkeepers, however, had watches to sell. As always, we were on the lookout for products we hadn't seen during our shopping expeditions. I found clear fingernail polish in a store called Tots and Teens, which also sold adult women's clothes and accessories. Ed gave the clerk an EC $10 bill, thinking it was a 5, the cost of the polish. As we were descending some steep steps from the store, the clerk came running after us to tell us we'd overpaid and handed Ed the other $5.

Stopping to buy a cold soft drink in one of the island's many liquor stores, we learned from the owner that economic times had been bad over the past several years, for Montserratians as well as tourists. His business was down 60 percent, he said. We had observed that would-be Christmas shoppers weren't really buying anything, but were just listening to music, walking around and talking to their friends.

After drinking our "Bentley," a lime-flavored soft drink from Trinidad, we had dinner at the Attic, an open-air restaurant up some dark steps across the street from Tots and Teens. The Attic was famous for its "roti," an island dish somewhat like a burrito, in that it was a filling wrapped in dough. Like similar dishes in many cultures, it could be eaten on the run without utensils. The first "roti" I ate was filled with beef and potatoes, but the Attic also had vegetarian or chicken varieties. I later learned that the chicken roti invariably had bones mixed in. This dish, like many other customs and foods in the Caribbean, comes from East Indians, many of whom, also being part of the British Commonwealth, settled in the islands as shopkeepers and restaurateurs.

Special foods were part of the Montserratian Christmas Eve celebration, much as in the USA, where some people put a glass of milk and cookies on the hearth for Santa. I asked Nicole at the pottery studio what a "jumbie table" was. I knew it was connected somehow with Christmas because I had heard a radio announcer read an advertisement about Christmas food and admonished Montserratians to "buy some for your jumbie table."

Nicole said it was the custom to set a table with plates of old-time food, sorrel and ginger beer to drink, pigeon peas and souse (made from a pig's head and feet, among other things, which I didn't want to know about) to eat. In the night, it was said, jumbies would come to eat the food, but not otherwise bother the home's inhabitants. Being a good Anglican, Nicole said she had never seen evidence that jumbies had visited her house, but she couldn't prove they hadn't. She said the family ate the food on Christmas Day if, in fact, it was still on the table in the morning.

I asked Cissie if she had ever seen a jumbie. "Only one," she told me. One night, when she was a child, Cissie said she was outdoors in the north of the island and saw a being all in white hovering about six or eight feet above the ground. She ran home as fast as her short legs would carry her and told her father what she had seen. He told her it was a jumbie, but not an evil one because it was white. She should run away from a black jumbie, if she ever saw one of those, he said. Nicole, overhearing this, made some comment about Cissie's light skin color, as if to say a very black person would not necessarily believe that a black jumbie was bad, and a white jumbie, benevolent.

The Bethel School, which had been unroofed in the hurricane of 1989 and had just been rebuilt after several years as an empty shell, was the scene of a celebratory Christmas program. The year before, we had attended the event in an estate-era stone building which the Methodist church established as a school in the 1830s. This school, like other Methodist-sponsored schools on the island, became public in 1930.

Earlier in the afternoon, we had been asked by two small village boys if we were going to come and hear them sing. They seemed shocked but pleased when we said we were. As we approached the school, we noted that all the children, who were assembling in the parking lot and on the steps, were wearing their uniform—pale blue shirts or blouses, beige pants on the boys and dark blue skirts for the girls. The local-access television station truck rolled up, and a technician began to set up his equipment.

There was no separation of church and state or political correctness on Montserrat. Nearly all the songs the children sang were religious—and all Christian at that. Interspersed with the music, sung with a gusto unknown in American schools, except perhaps in kindergarten before children know they're supposed to have stage fright, were poetry and dramatic recitations. One skit, which featured a junior high girl dressed as a mother and her two children, was largely unintelligible to us because she spoke in dialect. We could see, however, that the audience, which was made up primarily of women, liked it very much, particularly when the mother whacked the little boy who played the son.

A fashion show, in which children modeled clothing accompanied by recorded music, concluded the program. The audience really came to life then, as people stood to see better and clapped their hands and wiggled their hips in time to the music. Margaret, who was sitting next to me, became so disgusted with this display that she announced quite sternly, "I'm going home." Because we couldn't see a thing, we did, too.

As Barb Henry once said to me in mock dialect, to explain Montserratian behavior I didn't understand, "Is not we culture."

December 25 didn't seem like Christmas. We opened gifts sitting on our porch two steps up from our swimming pool. One year, I bought Ed a leather bag, which I laughingly referred to as a "purse." Most Montserratian men carried such bags, which were about 5 x 8 inches and had a wrist strap. Nobody thought them weird or feminine. I thought carrying such a bag while doing business in town made a lot of sense. You could carry more than you could in your pockets, and your pants wouldn't stretch or split. For my Christmas gift, Ed selected a woodcarving of a native woman.

Later that day, William brought us a gift in a brown paper sack. It was warm, so I knew he had been busy with his cutlass. When I opened the sack in the kitchen later, I saw that I had been given an entire goat leg minus the foot but with the liver, kidneys and part of the backbone and windpipe attached. This was too much for me right at lunchtime, so I wrapped my quarter of the goat carcass in the sack and covered it as best I could with an opaque plastic bag. After I ate, carefully steeling myself, I found Ed's hacksaw and the cutting board, intending to saw the leg off from the knee down and from the top of the haunch up, with the hope that I could keep the disgusting organ meat wrapped in the sack so I couldn't see it. Unfortunately, the hacksaw I had chosen wouldn't cut anything. Neither would the kitchen shears, the bread knife or a butcher knife.

Ed had a brilliant idea. He laid the green door he had removed from the pool house on the ground in the back yard, put the goat meat on it and attacked it with his own cutlass. This was exactly how William cut up meat, which was why it was always laced with shards of bone. In Ed's case, the problem was a bit different. The door was somewhat rotten. And I think his cutlass needed sharpening. Ed had to give the "roast" several hard whacks—sending meat and bone fragments flying—before he was able to separate that which I considered to be the "good" meat from the disgusting entrails.

After all this was done, and Ed was standing sweating and panting in a corner of the kitchen, I wrapped the good meat, in which green paint chips from the door were embedded, and stuck it into the freezer. I would cook it later, probably much later.

We had made it a Christmas ritual to drive up to Sharon's to take gifts and cookies. Sharon's Tanty (aunt) Polly, who was staying on Montserrat while recovering from surgery, told us that a representative of the government of St. Kitts had just called to wish her well. Oddly, she referred to St. Kitts, where she was employed in the school system, as "overseas," even though it was only about 55 miles away and could be seen on a clear day. Americans would call France "overseas," but probably not Nassau.

Sharon served us "sorrel," a red drink made by soaking the red blossoms of the sorrel plant with ginger and cloves. Some people enhanced the color with red food coloring, and everybody added a lot of sugar. Katy had been selling plastic bags full of sorrel blossoms, but I didn't know what to do with them so didn't buy any.

A woman we didn't know dropped by. Tanty told her they were offering lemonade and sorrel to their guests, but if the woman wanted hard liquor, she could serve herself. The woman immediately poured herself one glass of Harvey's Bristol Cream and then another. The gossip turned to the cancellation by the island's premier calypso and soca singer, "Arrow," of his Christmas night concert on the island. Arrow, whose real name was Alphonsus Cassell, performed all over the world and was often off-island, although he maintained a big house on Montserrat, called "The Palace."

Rumors abounded as to the reasons he would not sing. The women listed them and tried to decide which they believed. 1. Arrow is in Morocco. 2. He is on the island attending his sister's 25th wedding anniversary celebration. 3. He wants a government subsidy for his show, but the government has no money to pay him. 4. Instead of performing in Sturge Park for the masses at EC $20 a ticket, Arrow has said he will sing at the Montserrat Golf Club for an exclusive group who will pay more. The women could not decide whether one of those options was the truth or whether there was some other reason, but Tanty did say with certainty that no matter how big a star Arrow became, he would always be known to her by his childhood name: "Fonzi."

The day after Christmas, it was the custom for the island to hold the festival queen contest in Sturge Park, and one year we were more interested than usual because a girl from Bramble, a little village on our side of the island near Bethel, was a candidate. Her costume was constructed by Barb Henry, who had flown to the island to work on it from Antigua, where she was living and working as a photographer. The costumes, elaborate and large, required metal superstructures, so the contestant was encircled by the whole get-up and didn't really "wear" it in the traditional sense. This meant that practice in manipulating the costume was necessary. Without a period of practice, the costume could go off in one direction and the contestant, in another.

Added to the costume situation on this particular occasion was a howling wind blowing in from the sea, not to mention the late beginning of the pageant. By the time all the candidates had performed their talent numbers, it was midnight, and we hadn't yet seen the wondrous costumes on exhibit.

The ultimate winner in the talent stood out by contrast: she gave a humorous treatise on politics, partly in dialect, thus stealing the show. The costume also was fantastic—fruits and huge hibiscus blossoms with butterflies on flexible rods. The fabric which made the giant fruits had been hand painted to simulate reality. We left the contest soon after midnight with appearances by the candidates in formal wear and questioning by the judges still to come. The next day, we learned from the Henrys that the festival queen wasn't named until 3 a.m.

Sometime between Christmas and New Year's, we received a call from the Henrys that some dancers would be in the neighborhood, and we were invited to watch them perform. The dancers, men of all ages from teen to over 80, were called "whip dancers" by the expatriate residents and "masquerade dancers" by Montserrations. They danced in costume, to the accompaniment of percussion and fife, a tradition thought to have originated in the 1700s. With slight variations in costumes, music and dance steps, troupes also perform this sort of dance on other Caribbean islands.

Steps for the dances, copied maybe from what slaves saw while peeking through the windows of their masters' homes, were passed down from old men to young boys in order to keep the tradition alive. An 80-year-old man who walked with a cane when he wasn't dancing seemed to be the one the young boys looked up to, but "George," who lived in Harris', was the leader.

Although Montserratian men were in every way macho, the costumes seemed quite feminine—three-quarter length pants, always made of a print material and edged with lace, and the top, which looked like short-sleeved pajamas decorated with ribbons and bits of mirror. On their heads, the dancers wore tall hats resembling a pope's or an archbishop's miter. The hats were made of cardboard covered with wrapping paper, and the men also wore masks made of window screen painted with women's faces. I noticed that some of the faces had rings in the noses. According to Montserratian historian Howard A. Fergus, the ring denotes the captain of a particular masquerade troupe.

Like the dance steps, the costumes were the slaves' versions of the finery the estate owners wore to fancy balls in the 1700s, when sugar cane plantations fueled a lavish lifestyle, even on this remote Caribbean island. The plantation houses that remained on island were in ruins when we were living there. No sugar, limes or cotton were being grown on the island. And slavery had been abolished in 1834.

Adding to the idea of master and slave in the dancing was the presence of a long whip, which a dancer cracked periodically. Some said the whips were meant to chase away "jumbies," the spirits of the dead. Dance steps were reminiscent of the quadrille and the reel, and the songs played for the demonstration that we saw included "It's a Long Way to Tipperary" and "The Battle Hymn of the Republic." Percussion instruments were a drum made from a large can covered with goat hide, a tire rim which was hit with a stick, and a Carnation evaporated milk can full of pebbles. The fife was what I would call a tin whistle.

Gladys Henry said that the whip dancers were becoming an endangered species for several possible reasons: Young boys no longer saw the importance of keeping the tradition alive. They didn't want to be reminded of their slave past. They were too busy with other activities. They didn't care to practice. Fife players, particularly, were in short supply. Sometimes masquerade troupes on Montserrat were forced to import a fife player from another island when a performance was coming up. This day's fife player told me an effort was being made by the older men to recruit new dancers and musicians.

After several numbers, the whip dancers told us goodbye and walked up the hill toward Bethel, the next stop on their entertainment rounds. It was customary, Gladys said, for troupes to go to several villages sometime during the Christmas season, and island-wide festivals at that same time also featured performances.

A New Year's Day parade in downtown Plymouth was an annual event, and, of course, we drove over to see it. Neighbors told us it would be useless to get there before 4 or even 4:30 p.m. as the floats and bands wouldn't be organized until then. We were a bit over-eager the first time, perhaps because we did not fully understand "island time." We left our house at 3 p.m., which put us in town at 3:30 p.m., thinking we would be sufficiently late. Parade-goers already were lined up along George Street from the hospital down the mountainside to the sea, a distance of perhaps as much as four city blocks. We could tell when the parade was approaching by the increasing loudness of the music coming from those giant speakers.

The parade was led by a large jumbie wearing a green skeleton mask and a black cape with a hood. The other thing I noticed when he headed over to us to shake our hands was that he was very drunk. So were a lot of the people who danced in the streets behind the floats. All the bars were open to keep the momentum going. An old man with a white beard, also drunk, began to harass Ed, calling him "the white professor" because of Ed's beard.

Sharon, who was standing next to us with Medford, said we might have to move to get away from him, but she never said anything to the drunk directly. It's his profession, she said, to hang out on street corners and be drunk. I said he needed treatment, which she agreed, but she said there were no such facilities on the island. Sound trucks with their enormous speakers were interspersed with marchers and dancers, some in costume and scripted, others, ad hoc performers, who just joined the parade whenever they felt the urge. I never saw anybody grimace or cover their ears to shut out the blaring music. After the parade, I did hear some older people complain, saying that the young people wouldn't have eardrums left by the time they reached adulthood.

The parade was a blast and not just from the speakers. We saw everybody we knew and more, too. People were hugging each other and wishing their friends and relatives a Happy New Year and talking about the successful festival season, now complete as the parade disappeared down Marine Drive. Down by the War Memorial, where some more speakers had been set up, several hundred people remained behind to dance. We sat on the wall by the waterfront, listening to the music and watching the sun go down on another wonderful day in paradise.

St. Patrick's Day was a big deal on Montserrat, not because the island was settled by Irish fleeing persecution on St. Kitts, but because of a slave uprising. So it should not have been surprising that many Montserratians were upset that a "freedom run," meant to commemorate that uprising, was won one winter, not by an islander, but by a white guy from Arkansas, a student at the American University of the Caribbean.

That school, in Amersham, a village on the mountainside above the capital, was the training ground for physicians, some of whom had been denied entrance into medical school in the States and some who just wanted to go to school in the tropics. One particular Montserratian had won the "freedom run" for several years, and the deejay on Zed Jay Bee could hardly believe that a young white man had out-run him.

18
FAMOUS VISITOR

Probably the most exciting social event of our four winters on Montserrat was the visit of Prince Philip, consort of Queen Elizabeth of England. Many of the Canadians and Brits that lived on the island or had winter places there were invited to parties on the royal yacht *Britannia*, or as I called it, HRY (Her Royal Yacht), and to the Montserrat governor's residence. The governor and the chief of police were British. The chief minister of the island was a Montserratian.

Some Montserratians such as our friend Tony James, who earned an important British Empire Medal after Hurricane Hugo, were also invited to the receptions and parties. An Australian couple who operated a gift shop in downtown Plymouth would be among the guests as well. Americans were not on the guest lists.

Many of the Montserratians were totally enamored with all things royal. William and Mamie, for example, proudly displayed commemorative plates of Princess Diana and Prince Charles' wedding and of Queen Elizabeth's coronation. On the other hand, some of the royals' subjects were less than thrilled with the decorum required: curtsying and bowing and not shaking hands unless a hand is offered. In fact, a Canadian friend called the protocol "poppycock in this day and age."

According to the advance publicity, Prince Philip would arrive on the island via the royal yacht at 8 a.m. on a particular Sunday, attend an ecumenical church service, be the honoree at a reception and then attend a cricket match in Sturge Park. His arrival was discussed almost as much as the month-long lack of brown sugar. This was a situation, but not a problem.

After picking green beans on this auspicious morning and taking

Wishard for a walk around our yard, we changed clothes and headed for town so we could see HRY bearing HRH (His Royal Highness) "steam into Montserratian waters," as the newspaper put it that week. We were just in time to see the yacht, which looked like a rather large cruise ship, sailing north past the island's temporary jetty as we descended the mountainside into Plymouth. The jetty, built after Hurricane Hugo because the permanent one was destroyed, wasn't large enough to handle the yacht, so it maneuvered into position to anchor off-shore. We watched all this from the second floor balcony of a building owned by Arrow, the Soca King.

The streets were nearly deserted when we arrived in town at precisely 7:30 a.m., but soon people began arriving to witness the spectacle of the yacht, flying the Union Jack, the British Navy flag and another banner, which turned out to be Prince Philip's personal colors, being escorted to its anchorage spot by the Montserratian police launch.

As the anchor was dropped on the HRY, at precisely 8 a.m., as had been announced would happen, a string of flags was quickly hoisted, and three smaller boats were lowered over the side. One of these, we noticed, had an extremely powerful motor. The first boat brought the Royal Marine Band director and returned to the yacht, carrying Montserrat's commissioner of police plus Rupert McMillan, the Montserratian chief minister.

All the Royal Marine Band members and their instruments were transported to the shore next, by sailors wearing white knee socks, shorts, T-shirts and sailor hats. All this took nearly an hour. Meanwhile, Ed and I and a group of other gawkers stood on a low wall near the waterfront, so as to better see the action, but a Montserratian policemen politely asked us to cross the street and position ourselves behind another low wall, which was about 50 feet away. In true Montserratian fashion, no one disagreed, no one privately grumped, and everyone immediately complied.

At our new vantage point, we were directly across the street from a hastily built reviewing stand made of PVC pipe painted red, white and blue. It was located between two temporarily erected flagpoles. At just before 9:45 a.m., some people in uniforms of various kinds moved into formation right in front of the crowd of about 1,000, presumably so they could be reviewed by Prince Philip, who we assumed would be standing at some point on the reviewing stand. This group included the Girl Guides in neatly pressed shirts and skirts, their male equivalent, and the Montserrat defense force carrying semi-automatic weapons. The police, wearing white tunics, black pants, white helmets and swords, also participated. The officers carried swagger sticks.

A band, led by dentist Lenroy Masters, assembled immediately in front of us. The rag-tag group with their dented instruments wore khaki uniforms and red berets. Their sound resembled that of a seventh-grade band in the United States.

Soon, the British governor of the island arrived at the waterfront in a government car, which had his flag unfurled on the right front fender as it always did when he was a passenger. Next, the small boat with the big engine came dashing across the sparkling water from the *Brittania*. Masters' band played a discordant version of "God Save the Queen," and Prince Philip, wearing a brown suit and a straw hat, disembarked. Walking with his hands behind his back, as was his custom, he was joined by a group of dignitaries along Marine Drive, the street along the water, and together they made their way to the reviewing stand.

We were probably 50 feet away from Prince Philip. No one checked anyone's camera to make sure it wasn't a disguised gun. No one checked for bombs in anyone's purse or satchel. We were never cordoned off. No one made us stay off the wall, onto which many climbed once the action started in front of us.

Prince Philip then walked down the lines of police, defense force and various children's groups and talked to some of the people as he walked. We couldn't hear what he said, but nobody made any noise. When he walked around behind the little band so he could speak to Masters, the prince was about 25 feet away from us. We found this quite amazing.

Suddenly, the government car which had brought the British governor to the waterfront appeared, and he and the prince climbed in and sped away to the service at St. Anthony's Anglican Church. We had intended to attend this, but the church was closed to any more visitors at 10 a.m., and it was nearly 10. Instead, we walked up George Street to Peter's Mini-Mart, about three blocks away, to buy a soft drink. We knew it would be open, even on a Sunday, unlike other stores on the island.

Just as we arrived, it began to rain, and we stood under the eaves of the market to drink and to eat a candy bar. Since the church service was being broadcast over Zed Jay Bee, Radio Montserrat, we walked back to our car to listen. Quentin Plum, the minister of our Bethel Methodist Church, was the leader of the liturgy, and Prince Philip himself read a passage from the Gospel of John.

The rain let up just about the time the church service ended, and we walked back to the War Memorial for a concert put on by the Royal Marine Band. It was due to begin at 11:45, and we were able to find a great seat on a nearby wall. A woman, walking with one crutch because of what looked like a hip problem, sat on the wall beside us. Her name was Rachel, she said. Many white people seemed to know her and stopped by to shake her hand. She told us she often went to services at St. Anthony's Anglican and that she had attended the just-ended service with Prince Philip. "I've seen Prince Philip twice before," she said, her hazel eyes sparkling. "One time, he shook my hand and asked me my name."

The band members seemed uneasy in the heat, dressed as they were in white dress uniforms with red sashes, but they played with bravado, nonetheless, as the tropical sun beat down. Sweat rolled down their faces.

We had intended to watch the cricket match where Prince Philip was to make an appearance, but it was hot and we were hungry so we opted for lunch at home and a swim in our pool. As we returned home, William told us there had been a blessed event while we were away. "Nice Girl," our favorite goat, had "just finished" giving birth to twins. To neighbors fed up with roaming livestock, the fact that goats habitually had twins seemed ominous indeed, but we city slickers were sufficiently enthralled with anything related to farm life that we were excited about any and all newborns.

The neighbors' complaining was about to bear fruit, perhaps not huge baskets of fruit, but fruit nonetheless. William, a Mr. Baker and Mother Jackson, whose beige cow decimated our bananas and green beans when it jumped over our fence, were building a new pen on land given them by the government. It was located "on the other side of the ghaut," meaning just to the south of our neighborhood and nearly out of sight, William said. It looked to us as if the farmers, some of them anyway, were reading the handwriting on the wall. Despite the fact that I like animals, I was glad to hear that the herds of loose eating machines might soon be a thing of the past.

Actually, it was the law that all animals must be tied, and William, Mr. Baker and Mother Jackson were not in compliance. The law said further that loose animals could be shot, but, so far, the law had not been enforced in "the East," which had the reputation is-land-wide for having an animal problem. I understood the farmers' need to pasture their animals, but the goats' destructiveness couldn't be overlooked. They ate maniacally, frenzied, as if they hadn't had anything to eat for months, and they could literally devour a good-sized croton bush in seconds, not to mention any other plant they could reach when standing on tip toes. Sheep, by contrast, usually concentrated on edibles that grew low-down—grass and weeds but not bushes.

It wasn't long after the sheep and goats of William and Mr. Bak-er were removed and put into the pen that William told us "Nice Girl" was missing. He suspected someone had stolen her, perhaps to butcher her for personal use or to sell. He told us he would never eat goat water in a restaurant because, he said, "You never know what you are getting."

We always slept with the windows open and were awakened one morning at 5:45 with William talking on the phone. "What a ting (thing)," he said. "What a ting." To whom could he be talking when it was barely light? At daylight, when we were all outdoors, William walked slowly up our road to tell us all his goats had gotten out of their pen, which he and Mr. Baker had built from galvanized roofing. It was a three-sided, crudely built affair with the open side at cliff's edge. Goats being goats, they apparently had made what I would call an "end run" and climbed down the cliff to freedom. What a ting. What a ting, indeed.

That may have been what happened earlier to "Nice Girl."

Plane travelers to Montserrat endured hair-raising landings. The pilot aimed for a cliff and then abruptly turned left to set down on the short little runway.

The traveler palm (right) and the coconut palm (left) partially hid our view of the ocean.

Hugo Houses made of termite-treated lumber were given to many whose homes were blown away.

Laundry hung outside smelled wonderful and brought back memories of childhood.

When the volcano erupted, red-hot rocks were an after-dark spectacle.

Paradise East had a gate to keep loose cows, sheep and goats out of our green beans and hibiscus. Ed is on the porch.

19
MOTHER OF INVENTION

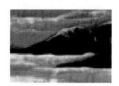

We bought our house "as is," which meant, among many other things, that the furniture was covered with '60s fabrics, now dingy and dirty. The foam rubber cushions had disintegrated, and, in some places, springs poked through. As I had not seen any foam cushions in any of the fabric or hardware stores, I wondered what islanders did when they wanted to reupholster their furniture. While enjoying a banana bread and tea break with Gladys and Vic Henry one day, I asked, figuring that the Henrys, who had lived on the island 20 years, would have suggestions.

Gladys said I could buy a foam mattress and cut it up for cushions, which was what she had done. Frankly, I was shocked. Of course, I could import furniture from the States or buy furniture on the island from its limited supply and throw away what was in our house. Importing furniture would be hideously expensive because of the shipping costs. That, I knew.

Gladys talked as if cutting up a mattress wasn't a horrible job, but she had an admonition: Cover the foam cushions with muslin to separate them from the "fashion fabric." That way, the heat would be less of a problem, whatever that meant. She added that, with our house shuttered in the summer, the inside temperature probably would rise to well over 100 degrees, and the humidity would be nearly the same. The "fashion fabric" she kept talking about would no doubt have to be purchased in the United States and brought with us on our next trip down. I had never seen upholstery fabric in any of the stores in downtown Plymouth.

We had a couch and three chairs that needed serious attention. I tried to imagine myself cutting up a mattress and decided I wouldn't be successful because all I had were a serrated bread knife, a nicked butcher knife and a utility knife with a razor blade. Besides those impedimenta, I didn't know what I was doing. The only alternative to the mattress might be foam, which we had heard was available sometimes from an obscure store called Tuitt's Universal, the name intended to imply that the store had everything. Actually, it did have a bit of this and a little bit of that—a couple of shower curtains, some Pyrex refrigerator dishes, cans of potted meat, lawnmower parts, packages of screws—and foam rubber if you could get the right thickness. But Tuitt's Universal was completely out of foam when we checked and didn't know exactly when a boat would come and replenish the supply. The upholstery project would have to wait.

The next fall when we returned to the island we went looking for foam again. Someone had told us the supply often was depleted by auto shops seeking to make seats for cars that were being driven until they fell apart. But we were in luck. We purchased 4 feet x 8 feet sheets of both 1-inch and 2-inch at Tuitt's Universal. The bill was EC $307—as opposed to EC $275 for a mattress we had no good way to cut up. We hoped that what we bought would be enough for at least two chairs.

I had estimated the amount of "fashion fabric" I would need, purchased it while I was home and brought it down in a large cardboard box. For a pattern, I painstakingly removed the old fabric and traced around it, one chair at a time. The result for the first chair was definitely amateurish, to say the least, lumpy and uneven. Next time, I knew I could do better.

We needed more foam when we next came down to the island from Indianapolis. I called Tuitt's Universal. The woman who answered the phone said she wouldn't have any foam until the following Monday at least because the shipment wasn't going to arrive by boat until Sunday. That Monday, we made a special trip to Tuitt's Universal to see if the "sponge," as it was called on Montserrat, had indeed arrived from the port and were thrilled to see that there were bales of the stuff on the porch. It was not yet unpacked, however, and the woman behind the counter said that she would see that a piece was cut and that it would be tied up and ready for us to take it, the next Saturday morning.

But the only foam found in the bales on the porch was 6-8 inch thick sheets and not 1-inch or 2-inch sheets, which is what we needed to complete our project. The woman behind the counter said that part of the shipment was probably in customs. We had learned much earlier that the sponge's being "in customs" might mean we couldn't procure any for several weeks. I was beginning to feel as if, in the grand scheme of things, I was not supposed to finish upholstering the chairs before we next went to Indianapolis and maybe never.

20
"BOCK-UP" AND COMING HOME

Getting ready to go "bock-up," for no matter how many months, was a hectic time. The following is a description of departure—the first year and also subsequently. In addition to packing, before departure we had to seal up all rice, noodles and dried beans in plastic or glass containers. Other expats had told me what to do, and I took the advice to heart. I had seen mouse droppings in our kitchen, and there was the debacle with the bean soup, although, realistically, the beans might have been infested before they were packaged at the factory.

Just when I was sealing up before the end of one of our winters, Sharon arrived with the $250 in American money Ed had asked to have converted from Eastern Caribbean Dollars to pay the Antigua veterinarian and various luggage handlers along our way to the States. She was undergoing a lot of stress at work, she said, because the bank where she worked was in the throes of "corporate restructuring." Four people already had been fired, and the staff was told to expect more "downsizing" in October, she told us. This was the only place Sharon had ever worked, ever since she was 18 years old. We felt very bad about this, and about leaving, too, but what could we do to help her?

The very morning of our flight home, while we were still stuffing possessions into our suitcases, Katy called at the gate. She was wearing a threadbare dress, so thin the print on the fabric had nearly worn away, a straw hat, and, astonishingly for her, she was carrying a purse. From the bottom of it, she extracted a jar of homemade guava jelly as a going-away present. She also had a collection of Canadian and American coins people had given her. "You can spend them, but

I can't," she said. We still had a few EC dollars, so we paid her what we could in exchange.

A little while later, William and Mamie arrived to say goodbye. Mamie asked me if she could have my garden hat, as hers was falling apart. I was glad to make her a gift of the old hat I'd been wearing, as I could buy another easily, and she could not. She said she finally needed to get her hair cut, after losing it all when she had chemotherapy for breast cancer. I knew she'd been sick, but had no idea what the problem was. In return for the hat, she gave me a going-away gift, too, a doily made by the nurse up at the clinic. Mamie went there every week, to be checked for "the pressure."

Although I knew it was silly, I walked around the garden then, silently saying goodbye to all our plants, the bananas which had struggled so hard to grow in the hardtack soil, the mango tree with its new grafts all wrapped in plastic and tape, the avocado bush in its wire cage to keep the lawnmower at a distance and the grapefruit and orange trees moving toward health after liberal doses of tender loving care and advice from Peter Smythe.

Gladys Henry told me once that "Rome is not built in a day" when I agonized about all the work I had to do when we returned to the island after a few months in the north. It wasn't only the weeds. The desirable plants also grew like mad; hibiscus could shoot up three feet, it seemed, in the blink of an eye. Slowly, as we left the island and returned season after season, I learned to pace myself, taking plenty of time to watch the birds and gaze at the sea.

When we, our animals and our luggage were aboard the puddle-jumper plane we chartered to take us to Antigua, Ed told me he had walked quietly into the back yard and pulled the plug on the swimming pool just before the taxi came to take us to the airport. Draining it while we were still in residence seemed so final, like a death.

Dr. Noah, the chief veterinarian, was not there to greet us at the Antigua airport and take our $100 USD, so we went into a coffee shop where we gloated over the possibility that we had escaped paying his "fee." But then a Montserrat Airways employee came looking for us. The old vet, bow-legged in his shorts, met us beside the pets' cages. He did not apologize, but complained that he didn't know we were coming. This wasn't true, as we had written him a letter telling him the date of our departure, and he had answered the letter. He had spent the whole morning, he said, processing a huge shipment of chicks, most of which had arrived dead. After looking briefly into Sunny's and Wishard's cages, he pronounced them healthy. "Now," he said, "there is the question of the money." Ed peeled off two $50 bills and handed them over. I was disgusted, but tried not to show it.

The weeks from mid-May to the first of December always passed quickly, and by the time we were packed and ready to go back to Montserrat, we knew why we went. There were no leaves on the trees in Indiana. The days—90 percent of them, it seemed—were cloudy and gray. By late November, the chill set in.

Before we arrived back on the island, usually after an eight-month hiatus, nearly all the plants, with the benefit of summer rains and warm, humid air, had grown mightily. Oleanders and hibiscus bushes hung over the front lawn, which also served as our driveway. Bushes across the front of the porch completely obscured our view of the ocean. Although our lawn had been cut, weeds and tall grass grew in all the flowerbeds. Always, for unknown reasons, some plants, even some that were well established, failed to survive. I would try to figure out what I had done or not done that caused them to die. I was never able to. The condition of the yard was quite depressing, but I told myself to be grateful that the skies were blue and there was no snow.

On returning to the island our third winter, Ed and I learned from Nancy that Mamie was very sick. She had been having dizzy spells and some weakness when we were still on island in the spring, but she thought she might just be a bit anemic. It was far worse than that.

The same day I heard this news I met Yvette Oliver, whom the Owensbys had hired as a nurse, walking down the road toward their house. She told me Mamie could no longer walk without help because one lung was being eaten away by cancer. Under the circumstances, she had to have someone stay with her, as William needed to be busy with his animals, Yvette said. Mamie had gone to England during the summer while we were up in the States, and at the time, she was given just a few weeks to live. Doctors encouraged her to check into a hospice in London, but she said she wanted to go back to Montserrat. They told her to be quick about it, or she would be too sick to travel. That was in August.

When William appeared at our gate later that day and asked if we wanted to visit her, we went immediately. She was sitting in a chair in her bedroom, looking much thinner than I had remembered. And her salt and pepper hair, done up in braids, was no longer covered by a black wig. "God is keeping me alive," Mamie said. She had opted not to have chemotherapy, but Yvette told us later her son was sending her pain medication, acquired from doctors in England. Mamie assured us she wasn't in any pain.

We didn't stay long, and when we left, we invited William to ride into town with us, as we had grocery shopping to do. By the time we had driven a couple of miles out of Bethel, our passengers included not only William but also a woman we didn't know and Katy Connor. In town, we ran into a choir member who told us Quentin, the minister who was universally loved by all the choir ladies, had been transferred to Nevis. This reassignment of pastors after a few years is the Methodists' custom for its ministers. Called the "itinerancy system," this practice dates from the early days of the denomination and assures that every pastor has a church and every church has a pastor. So there was either sadness or joy in congregations every four to eight years or so. Our new minister's name was Marilyn Gerald.

As the days went by, more and more people stopped by the Owensbys' home to pay their respects to Mamie, who by then had begun to cough a lot and seemed to be having trouble getting her breath. She was 65 years old.

Things were not going well for some of our other dear friends. Sharon told us she had, indeed, been fired from her job. Because she had worked at the bank 20 years, she thought her longevity would keep her from being caught up in the "restructuring." She was matter-of-fact about this, but that was her usual reaction to everything. In fact, we were realizing more and more that stoicism seemed to be a Montserratian trait. Perhaps it was because we were still relatively new on the island and didn't know people well enough for them to share intimate thoughts.

Just after Christmas, we heard that Mamie was in a lot of pain, not mitigated very well by the medicine she was taking. We hesitated to keep dropping in so as not to tire her out, but we did want her to know that we cared about her. Helen said Mamie was barely responsive, perhaps because she had been given a lot of painkillers. I was beginning to realize we were not going to be able to take Mamie for a drive as she had wanted and as we had promised. It was too late. Her minister was visiting when we walked down to pay our respects later that day. Although William kept touching her face to try to awaken her, our friend slept on peacefully.

Quite shaken, I was stumbling up the road toward home when I met another of the neighbors, also coming to visit. It won't be long now, the neighbor said. William said her son would be arriving soon from England. When she was awake one day, Ed asked her if she would like some homemade strawberry yogurt, and she said she would. As it was difficult to carry ice cream or sherbet home from the grocery store without its melting, I started making frozen yogurt at home, using vanilla yogurt, fruit and condensed milk. To be really daring, I sometimes made chocolate yogurt with Hershey's syrup, walnuts, vanilla yogurt and milk. It didn't click with me for several months why Ed and I were both gaining weight.

Mamie's son, Sherman, arrived on island to see his mother before she died. "I've been crying a lot," he told us, in confidence, "but I can't let her see it." He was angry because she had been such a creative person, making all those dresses and beautiful wedding cakes. And now her life had come to this. It wasn't fair, he said. When she retired in England, she and William had returned to Montserrat to enjoy the money they had saved.

A Ford employee in London, Sherman said his wife was born on St. Vincent, another Caribbean island. Like his mother and step-father, he would like to retire to Montserrat, build himself a house and buy a boat he could use to travel among the islands. Sherman was a busy guy. He was almost never at his mother's house, so I asked her if she was enjoying his visit. She wasted no time in answering: "I can't wait to see the back of him." When I asked her why, she said he was getting too many phone calls—and upsetting the quiet decorum of their house. "He knows a lot of people," she said, "and has met a whole lot more."

I asked her how she was feeling, and she replied, "You'll laugh at me, but I slept all day yesterday. I didn't even know Yvette was here. The tablets do that." I took that to mean she was heavily sedated most of the time. We had seen that ourselves.

About three days later, at 10 in the morning, William called us on the phone. "Mamie, she die," he said. "When?" I asked. Michael said she had stopped breathing about 30 minutes before. I took off at a run. When William saw me, he laid his head on my shoulder. "My Mamie gone," he wailed. "My Mamie gone." After I had comforted him as best I could, I went into the bedroom where she lay. Her eyes were closed, and a cloth strip had been placed like a sling under her chin and was tied on top of her head, presumably to keep her mouth closed. Although her face looked gray, she seemed at peace, lying with the sheet pulled up to her chest.

Yvette, who was sitting in the room with the body along with another woman I didn't know, said the nurse at the clinic had been summoned. I sat with the women, perhaps for a half hour, as they watched the body for signs of life. As William made more and more phone calls, more cars full of friends arrived. There was no sign of a doctor or the undertaker. The man from Irish's Funeral Home, the only one on the island, didn't arrive for two hours—at about 12:30 p.m. He was driving a black station wagon. It had no side curtains or tinted glass. Two men got out of the station wagon, one wearing shorts. They wheeled the body out on a gurney, wrapped in the sheet that had been under her on the bed. Mamie's son, Sherman, helped load the body into the back of the wagon. Then he and William followed it into Plymouth.

Life goes on. Soon after the cortege left, we, too, drove into town to see if we could find a brush for our vacuum cleaner. We knew it was a long shot, but what the heck? We persisted long enough to get a "no" from all the likely stores. No one had the slightest idea where to look; it was an item never seen on the island. One helpful suggestion was: "I guess maybe you will have to import one."

When we returned home, we realized that one car after another was passing our house on the way down the hill to the Owensbys'. Even when we went to bed at 10:30 p.m. we could still hear the hymns, clapping and laughing. The noise seemed to be louder after we turned out the lights, perhaps because everything appears magnified in the dark. I thought to myself, "So what. Your wife doesn't die every day of the week," and promptly went to sleep. I was awakened several times in the night, and at about 5:30 a.m. I heard several cars chugging up our hill. I wrapped a pillow around my ears.

Funerals in Montserrat were always held late in the day, after the sun started to go down, so I had time to make slaw and cook sweet potatoes for our dinner, which we would eat after we returned home. It had been raining off and on, a very funereal kind of day.

The funeral was to be held in the large Pentecostal church near downtown Plymouth because the tiny church where William and Mamie worshipped was too small for the crowds that were expected. As we passed through Harris', Katy Connor literally jumped out of a little house along the way. She was wearing a black skirt, white blouse and black hat, plus her wig. It was her funeral outfit, and she wanted a ride. We asked Katy if the body had been returned to the Owensbys' house last night for a wake. "No, no," she said, "there is a funeral home on the island now and the body stays there." Before there was a funeral home, though, the body stayed in the home until the funeral and burial, both of which had to be either the day of the death or a day after. When a person had a lingering illness and death was expected, Katy said, the family often made the coffin and had it ready.

The church was packed, as we suspected it would be. Helen, Ed, I and two other women were the only white people there. The casket was open. Because we were so far back in the church, I couldn't see much, but I did notice that Mamie was wearing a little lace cap on her head, the same sort of funeral headgear common in some European countries. In front of the casket was an enormous bouquet of cut flowers and a silvery sign which read "Mum."

The service included a lot of hymn singing, and even a solo by William, the bereaved husband. The person who read the eulogy told how Mamie's mother took her and her brother, who was then three years old, from Montserrat to Antigua on a sloop. Somehow, the boat went adrift or got lost and ended up in the Virgin Islands two weeks later. Mamie, the eulogist said, had spat into her brother's mouth to keep him alive.

After the funeral, we, along with many others, joined the motorcade through Plymouth to the cemetery, which was next to the soccer stadium along the waterfront. The grave had already been dug by the island's gravediggers, some weird men, who, Helen said, "aren't all there." We sang hymns, including "When the Roll is Called Up Yonder," while the gravediggers lowered the casket into the ground and shoveled dirt on top. There was no canopy or artificial grass, just the hole in the ground. Afterwards, those who had brought bouquets, some professionally made and some just a few handfuls of flowers from the garden, laid them on the dirt. As the service was concluding, the minister invited everyone to the Owensbys' house. Uh-oh, I thought, another late night. The custom was to pay the gravediggers with money and a bottle of rum. We heard countless times, but couldn't corroborate the story, about the Catholic funeral of a white man whose survivors didn't know about the payment custom. When they didn't produce the obligatory bottle of rum, the gravediggers ranted and raved in front of the mourners, saying that if they weren't paid properly, they would dig up the corpse.

In a short amount of time, we had another funeral to go to. I put on a new white blouse and a light blue skirt, the closest I had to an all-white outfit and walked up to the church to sing with the choir at the 3:30 funeral of Giles Sweeney, Evelyn's elderly father. Margaret Joseph wore a black straw hat with her black polka-dotted skirt and white blouse, and a prominent male high school teacher wore a black suit, which looked homemade. It was quite ill-fitting, but as the saying on Montserrat went, "He doin' the best he can."

The woman who owned the fence-jumping cow that wrecked our green beans also died during our winters on the island. And the choir was expected to show up for that funeral, which was scheduled for 4 p.m. Rain poured down just as I should have been leaving to walk up to the church, so Ed drove me; he didn't stay. The parishioners, including the choir, waited and waited for the service to start. An alto who sat next to me in the choir speculated that the powers that be didn't have the written permission required to bury the body. It turned out, however, that a niece, who was in charge of the funeral for the family, had the legal paper, but she hadn't yet picked up the flowers that were to be placed near the casket for the service.

At about 4:30 p.m., she walked into the church carrying a spray of carnations and a yellow heart made with flowers. Immediately, the pallbearers walked in with the casket, which looked to be made of gray cardboard. It was shaped like the stereotypical coffin—wide at the shoulders and narrowing at the feet. One pallbearer wore a knitted hat, and another carried an umbrella. Freddy Connor, who sang in the choir, was one of the pallbearers. Because he had a van, he also was chosen to drive the casket up the hill to the cemetery, which was behind the church. To fit the casket into his van, he had to leave the hatch door open. Although he had removed the back seat, the casket hung out the back end of the van quite a distance. I looked at that and the steep slope and the bumpy path that led up to the cemetery, and I whispered to two of the women, "Wouldn't it be awful if the casket fell out the back?"

Both of them got quite a kick out of this prospect and snickered into their hands. So much for honoring the dead. Freddy must have had the same thought. After trying to negotiate the first 50 feet of the path to the cemetery, he backed down and headed to the main road, turned right up the hill into Tuitt's Village onto the smoother road and around the corner, the long way but safer to the burial ground.

In our age bracket—the retirees and the downright elderly—death was a constant specter. Helen, who had been a vital part of the fourzies crowd and host of many parties and bridge games in Spanish Point, told us when we returned for our last winter on the island that she had been losing weight and was below 100 pounds. She was diabetic, we knew. I couldn't imagine that she was eating correctly and theorized her blood sugar might have been totally out of whack.

Coming home from a readers' theater play on the Westside late one night, she fell walking from our car to her front door and cut her head. There was no warning for this; she said her legs simply buckled under her. She told me she was due to go for a blood test in a few days, so she didn't see a need to seek medical attention any sooner. The day of the blood test she phoned to ask me to come down to her house just to be there while she took a shower. She was dizzy, she said. When I arrived, another neighbor, who was sitting on Helen's porch, told me she was being seen by a doctor inside the house at that very moment.

In a conference behind her house after the consultation, the doctor gave us the shocking news: he had felt a mass in her abdomen and believed that her weight loss and the jaundice she'd had for a while were likely due to pancreatic cancer. If she stayed on the island without treatment, he said, she might live three weeks. If she returned to Canada, she might last a couple of months. Although he hadn't told her the diagnosis, she knew she was very ill and said she wanted to go up north to be near her children.

The doctor did tell her she should go straight to the emergency room as soon as she landed in Toronto. Because Air Canada flew only on weekends, she would not be able to leave Montserrat for a week. During that time she wasn't to be left alone, so neighbors drew up a schedule of volunteer shifts. And Helen asked Wilma, a close friend, to fly with her as she felt too weak to navigate the trip back to Canada by herself. In addition, Wilma, who had moved into the empty house next door to us, volunteered to provide night shift care every night until time to fly. Many of the neighbors accompanied her to the airport on the day she left the island.

Helen had surgery in Canada and lived about a year. Her long-time yardman and his wife, who had become social friends over the years, adopted her dog. The yardman had given Helen his belt for the trip home because her slacks were so much too big they were in danger of falling off.

21
CHARITY

Lucy Evans, like many Montserratians, had worked in England for many years and returned to her homeland when she retired. She had been a nurse and did not stop caring for others when she was no longer officially employed. When we first met her, she had recently organized Meals on Wheels and was feeding about 25 people, using a van donated by the United Kingdom. She did all the cooking with an assistant, a woman in her 70s, and relied on volunteers to do the driving. Lucy was going slowly blind, whether from glaucoma or macular degeneration, but that did not stop her from her good works.

As time went on, Ed and I became more and more involved in the Meals on Wheels operation. Actually, Ed did much more than I did; he drove Lucy and Elizabeth Nichols, her assistant, and the food on many occasions, while I just went along for the ride and to observe. The British van broke down, so Ed and the other volunteers began driving their own vehicles.

On the Eastside of the island, it was usual to deliver meals in Tuitt's village up the mountain from Spanish Point and then in Harris' and Windy Hill, which were along the road to Plymouth on the Westside. In Windy Hill, Lucy asked if I wanted to go into a cabin with her so I could talk to the 94-year-old male occupant. He was not at home, but we went inside anyway. The house had three tiny rooms and no bathroom, as far as I could tell. The living room was furnished with three kitchen chairs and a small table, which was also the desk for the man's grandson, who, Lucy said, slept each night and did his homework there. This sort of living arrangement was one of the ways Montserratians looked after their at-risk relatives. Many trophies adorned the walls in the living room, won by the grandson in talent competitions and debate.

Lucy was a bit worried when she didn't find the 94-year-old at home, but she put his food on a plate along with a spoon and went looking for him in the immediate neighborhood. She found her client sitting on a nearby porch talking to another old man. Originally, we had been scheduled to make deliveries for her the day before, but she cancelled Meals on Wheels on that day because a man in Tuitt's died. As he had no relatives on the island, Lucy and Elizabeth had gone to the mortuary, where he was "on ice." They washed and dressed him for the funeral.

Lucy said she got the names for new Meals on Wheels clients in a variety of ways—mainly through churches or social service clubs or agencies. A Catholic sister told her about one old man in the south part of the island. According to the nun, he always begged cigarettes from the priest who took him Communion. Lucy said the man always asked her for cigarettes, too, and she scolded him about his habit.

She envisioned Meals on Wheels as a means of delivering not only food, but friendship and social work to an underserved or unserved population. For example, if a client was sick, Lucy could tell the proper authority. If a client needed laundry done or a bed to sleep on, she could either wash the clothes herself or provide a mattress herself or find someone to take care of these needs. When delivering meals a couple of weeks before, she discovered an elderly woman sleeping in her cabin on a pile of rags. That occurred in Tuitt's, one of the poorest settlements on the island.

Lucy's cooking was delivered five days a week and was intended as the main meal of the day. It usually consisted of a stew or soup, a drink and "a bit of bread." We often took along a cooler filled with ice, so recipients could have ice in their drinks.

One client, who lived downtown in Plymouth, was diabetic, and before Meals on Wheels, she ended up in the hospital at least once a month with her insulin levels askew. That's because she would get hungry and walked across the street to a grocery store, where she bought cakes and bread to fill up on. Since Meals on Wheels, Lucy said, the woman had not once gone to the hospital.

I learned surprising things about the way poor people coped. One little old man who lived in Long Ground walked down to Tuitt's, probably a mile away, to pick up his food. Actually, he hobbled down the mountain as he had a bad foot. This was the same man who always carried his spoon because he didn't want to wait to eat until he returned home. Instead, he sat on a fire hydrant to wait for the Meals on Wheels van and had his lunch right there. Lucy chided the man when she found out he recently had walked all the way up to the soufriere to dig sulfur to sell. "You could topple over up there, and no one would find you," Lucy told him.

Also in Tuitt's, we sometimes gave meals to Mu-Mu, her brother Billy and their chronically ill mother. One day as we drove up the mountain, we saw Mu-Mu herself walking along holding the hand of a very pretty little girl. We had heard Mu-Mu had a boyfriend in Farms Village, and lately we had observed her heading to and coming from there. She was always carrying a paper bag. I'd also heard she wouldn't be attending choir practice very much because she was otherwise occupied, whatever that meant.

Lucy seemed surprised we knew all about the boyfriend. Mu-Mu used to have a boyfriend "on Antigua", Lucy said, but she threw him over for the one in Farms. To complicate the situation, the pretty little girl, the daughter of the Antiguan boyfriend, had been staying temporarily with Mu-Mu. Needless to say, she couldn't take the child with her to Farms.

Driving on toward Plymouth, we arrived in the village of Dyer's, where we made a sharp right turn and a steep dip in the road past the Seventh-day Adventist Church. After the road plunged steeply, it rounded a bend and began climbing again, past banana trees in the secluded lower lands and then up, up, up to the remote village of Molyneaux.

In previous weeks, we had left the Molyneaux food with a woman in Dyer's, and she took it up the mountain. That woman, however, was on maternity leave. Lucy said she was afraid the food might not get to the people who needed it unless we took it ourselves. The lush foliage in Molyneaux gave way to ever drier conditions as we drove down into Plymouth and then to the arid south, where goats outnumbered human beings and trees were scarce.

When we had made our food deliveries for the day, we returned to Plymouth. At the wharf, the man who sold fresh fish had gathered a large crowd by blowing into a conch shell. Lucy and Elizabeth asked to be let out of the car to make a purchase, and we arranged to meet them afterward outside of Papa's supermarket, one of the other grocery stores on the island. Montserratians preferred doing business with Papa's because management there gave away food after Hurricane Hugo.

When I say "fresh fish," I say it tongue in cheek. There were no live wells in most of the fishing boats and no ice aboard, so by the time the fish ended up in the truck for sale, they were quite dead and stiff. What the fishmonger was selling that particular day was trunk-fish, a weird triangular-shaped beast with a rigid carapace. These strange fish are found along reefs in the tropics and are about 8 inches long. Some people are allergic to them. Driving back to Spanish Point when everyone's shopping was finished, we added William to our riders. He'd been shopping, too, so our car was filled to the top with people and sacks of groceries. I carried a plastic bag of raw eggs on my lap. Eggs were sold by the half dozen and always sent home in plastic bags.

The drama of Mu-Mu continued. Our little band of Meals on Wheels helpers came upon her slowly climbing the hill toward Tuitt's on our next service day. Although she normally had short, reddish hair, she was wearing woven-in dreadlocks, which were black. I assumed she had herself fixed up this way because she had taken up with a Rasta. Lucy was shocked that Mu-Mu might have paid money to have her hair woven because her family was very poor.

Mu-Mu caused quite a stir the night of a choir concert in Harris' because on the way home she asked to be let out of Freddy's van in Farms. That's where we thought her lover of the moment lived. The stir resulted from two things: one, that she did not stay all night with her mother, who was disabled, and two, she still had her choir robe with her. In the eyes of some of the singers, this was a holy garment.

Many examples come to mind about how Montserratians looked out for each other. In Harris' one day while delivering Meals on Wheels, I went to Beebe's Bakery to buy soft drinks for Lucy; Elizabeth, Lucy's assistant; Ed, and me because it was a very hot day. The woman behind the counter was asking a little girl, who looked to be about 8 years old, what her mother had given her for lunch. The little girl said, "Nothing." The store was full of children, all dressed in their school uniforms and all between 6 and 10 years old. The woman, without making a fuss, broke off a big piece of the banana she was eating and gave it to the hungry child.

Some days, we encountered more crazies and drunks than usual on our Meals on Wheels route. Up in the village of Molyneaux, we had parked our car next to a bar so Lucy could deliver a meal to an arthritic old woman. A man came staggering out of the bar and announced that he was born in 1927. "Are you English?" he asked Ed.

"No, we're American," Ed told him, whereupon the man asked for a dollar. When Ed told him no, the man said, "You're a son of a bitch." Lucy, who by that time was back in the car, told Ed to drive on.

In another village, an equally drunk man approached the car and asked Lucy to buy some of the beans he had raised in his garden. She inquired about the price, and he told her $5. When she told him that was too much money for so few beans, he began ranting and cursing, saying she had plenty of money because she was paid by the government. Lucy said many Montserratians thought Meals on Wheels was a government program and then treated her badly, wanting more than she could provide. "Some of them treat me like a servant," she said.

Because Meals on Wheels was an ad hoc operation, Lucy used all sorts of containers for the food—whipped topping and soft margarine tubs were favorites. For drinks, she used empty plastic soda bottles with screw caps. We and other people in Spanish Point saved containers for her. When she delivered the meals, she brought back the tubs and bottles that food was delivered in the day before. Sometimes, the clients washed those dishes, and sometimes they didn't.

Not all Montserratians, sad to say, were good to their elderly relatives. Some of the clients had children living on the island, Lucy noted, but they "don't do anything for their parents. I never thought I'd see that on Montserrat." Lucy thought nothing of contacting the children and berating them, if she thought they were being derelict in their duties. One old man, for example, had no running water in his house and hence no way to wash his clothes unless he carried them to an outdoor spigot several hundred yards away. His daughter lived within walking distance, Lucy said, but had not volunteered to help. So Lucy gave her a lecture.

As time went on, there was a push to institutionalize Meals on Wheels. Lucy had been providing the service as a volunteer, but she was getting older and losing her sight. Vic Henry said the nurses' residence next to the clinic in Bethel had been promised as the headquarters for the feeding program, and a refrigerator, freezer and stove had been donated, or soon would be. Henry hoped that some day there would be more than one kitchen preparing meals for the old people.

The goal, he said, was to feed between 100 and 125 indigent, old people. So far, about all Lucy could handle was 25, using her own kitchen. She provided the food herself, although my understanding was that she received some donations. In addition to her Monday through Friday Meals on Wheels, Lucy also provided low-cost, home-baked bread for the poor people who lived in the villages of the East, a continuation of what her mother had done for nearly 70 years. Her mother stopped baking bread in 1978 when she went completely blind, Lucy said.

She baked on Saturdays in the same stone oven with a cast-off galvanized roof that her mother had used. It was located beside the small house of the mother, who was 99 when she died. Her house; the oven, and another small building, which was used as a kitchen, were being kept by Lucy as a memorial to her mother. Although Lucy Evans had been raised by a relative on Trinidad (Why, I never learned) and then had a nursing career in England, she returned to Montserrat and learned from her mother how to make bread "in the old way."

We arrived to watch the baking operation and to take pictures to send to our granddaughter just as Lucy was ready to put the first batch of loaves into the oven. "Logan," who had worked at the bakery since he was a child, tended the wood fire, which had been lit some time earlier. With his years of experience, he knew exactly when to push the coals off to the side. Then, using a long-handled, homemade paddle, he slid the loaves, each on its own piece of banana leaf, into the oven. After the loaves were all loaded, he pushed a worn, wooden door over the front opening.

Meanwhile, in the kitchen shack, Lucy and Elizabeth readied more loaves, from flour purchased in 100-pound bags and yeast sent from England. Lucy said Montserrat had no "proper" yeast. The little kitchen, which had crude wooden tables for mixing and kneading, didn't have running water or electricity, but there was a "pipe" just outside and a stone sink.

Elizabeth, too, had worked at the bakery since she was little. For this occasion, she wore a knitted hat and a flowered dress, but no shoes. Some little boys stopped by the oven to purchase bread, carrying their own plastic bag to put it in. The leg of one of the boys was completely covered with gauze. When we asked about him later, Lucy said he had been burned when gasoline he'd been pouring into a "coalpot" spilled on his skin and ignited when he struck a match.

He was sitting on the ground with the coalpot between his legs at the time. These charcoal pots were used for cooking in many poor families without electricity or the money to buy propane for a stove. Years before, this was the only means of cooking on the whole island, and many people had burn scars. Right away, I could think of three women just from my acquaintances.

When Lucy and Elizabeth had baked the plain loaves, they made special coconut bread, so buyers could have "something sweet," Lucy said. Elizabeth, who was 70-ish at the time and rawboned, sat, legs wide apart, on the steps to the kitchen shack, grating coconut meat into a bowl. Her gnarled hands moved so swiftly I was sure she would bark a knuckle any minute, but she never did and in a short time had an entire coconut processed into slivers.

One coconut wasn't enough. So Logan took another from a tree in the yard and smashed it against the sink. He drank the coconut milk, obviously a perk enjoyed by the bakery helper, before picking up a large butcher knife with which to cut out the coconut meat. This was accomplished with just a few strokes of the knife.

22

UNHAPPY DAYS

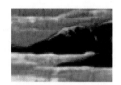

After the Mabrys went back to Canada, there was tribulation in the choir. Being an outsider, I didn't really understand what was going on for a while. Walter Lee, the retired music teacher, began to lead the little band of singers, some of whom quite obviously disliked him. Others didn't seem to care who was in charge. Lee sang loudly and off pitch, but he was earnest.

He never started choir practice on time. The women knew this would happen, so they didn't arrive on time either. Paul Mabry would have been fuming. Lee told us we would henceforth sit in the choir loft for practice, not in the pews down front as we'd been doing before Paul left. Even that was enough to set off members of the choir.

When one of the women arrived—late—she said she wanted to sit in the pews. We'd already started practicing, sitting in the choir loft, so one of the altos said she thought we ought to stay where we were. The late-comer said, without smiling, "You should keep your mouth shut."

The alto answered, "I don't have to. This is a free country, and I'm allowed to have my own opinions."

Lee kept telling us how "things are done at Trinity," the mother church of Methodism on the island, located in Plymouth. He had been worshipping there for some time, although he used to be a member of the Bethel church. He also compared how things were at present in the Bethel church compared to how they used to be in some golden age in the past. Naturally, the women hated this. I made a decision that if he were the choir director the next winter season, I was going to quit. The organization of the rehearsals was chaotic, the women were fighting among themselves and they were disrespectful of him. I didn't need the aggravation.

The summer came and went, and we and our pets returned to the island for the winter season. Who would be leading the choir? When the Mabrys returned, our routine at the Bethel church began again with Paul in charge. After choir practice one week in December that year, Marilyn Gerald sat down with the choir to discuss "some problems" that had recently arisen. Paul had told her about absences and tardiness and the time our one bass refused to sing on Sunday morning, but sat in the pews.

Those who attended the meeting sat impassively, and no one said anything. The tardiness problem was severe, but I doubted Marilyn's meeting with the choir would have any effect, not when one considered the lateness of that last New Year's parade. It was supposed to start at 2 p.m. and didn't until nearly 5 p.m.

The minister wanted Margaret to phone the absent and the late and try to get them to mend their ways. This seemed to me to be a lot like grade school tactics. As time went on, it became clear to me that there was a constant struggle going on between Paul Mabry and Lee. During the announcements after one choir practice, Lee announced to the choir—with Paul Mabry standing there—that an all-island Palm Sunday evening concert was being planned, and our choir was going to take part. There would be some expense, he said, as he wanted the women to have long black skirts and white blouses.

I questioned where we would wear such a costume after the concert, and Adele announced that she had "no interest" in a black skirt. Besides, she said, we had just made new choir robes for ourselves. And Margaret had yet to be reimbursed by everyone for that fabric. She said we needed to get the finances straightened out from the choir robes venture before launching into another one. At this discussion, Walter Lee said, "Well, let's forget the whole thing" and stalked out the door. My guess was that his snit would keep him from showing up Sunday for services and for many weeks to come. Was I wrong about Walter. He showed up to sing on Sunday and was quite subdued, although he sang off key and too slowly, perhaps his revenge.

All the choir members, except Alicia and me, wore blue collars with the robes on Sunday. She and I wore purple, which was the color we had been wearing for several weeks. We were told that the change in color was announced at the last choir practice, after the benediction. Alicia and I agreed that, with the Walter Lee problem, we hadn't even heard the benediction.

Adele Mabry confided that she wasn't aware of the color change either, but she and Paul were saved because they kept all the collars, purple, red, green and blue, in their car, just in case. Adele later said said there would indeed be a Palm Sunday concert but that Walter definitely would not be in charge. Paul had met with Walter to discuss the concert and informed him he could not unilaterally tell the women they had to have black skirts and white blouses for the occasion. Walter revealed that he himself already had such an outfit. Paul also told him he should have checked with the minister before he laid plans, which included asking several people to sing solos. Walter said that, henceforth, he wouldn't have anything to do with the concert.

A choir member told me that Lee had been practicing "The Lost Chord," before choir rehearsals, probably because he was planning to sing it during the Palm Sunday concert. When asked later if she was going to let Walter sing, the minister retorted, "Absolutely not." The person who overheard the clandestine rehearsals said Walter never found the lost chord.

On and on the Palm Sunday dressing perturbance went. In a complete turnaround, it was Paul who told Margaret what the choir would be wearing—robes for the first half of the concert, and then robes would be removed for the second half to show off an assortment of colorful dresses. "Doesn't everyone have a green dress?" Margaret wanted to know, somewhat plaintively, "It's Palm Sunday."

But the women couldn't bear to look different from each other, so it was decided they would wear robes for the entire concert rather than take them off to display their dresses. They would wear red collars and carry music in red folders. These decisions were difficult for the women to make; Margaret was only too happy to make them, going against her own idea that green would be the appropriate color to wear.

Adele wanted to know who would be in charge of the reception, which was to be held in the manse after the concert. A couple of the women said they didn't think anyone needed to be in charge. Adele said she would bring bar cookies, and I said I would bring cookies, too. As far as I knew, no one else was bringing anything. I wasn't sure if anything was planned to drink. When Adele's probing scraped up so little information, Paul said, "Well, maybe you don't want to have a reception."

"Yes, we do," the women said, but they still didn't volunteer to provide any leadership or food. Adele and I felt the same way: we didn't want to take over. It was their church and their island. We were just guests.

In addition to the future Palm Sunday concert, we were practicing for a concert commemorating Montserrat Electric's service to the island. There was no public electric service on Montserrat until 1955, and that was 12-hour-a-day electricity to Government House, the hospital and the streets of Plymouth. Private homes didn't receive electricity on that first go-round. In fact, many indigenous islanders were apprehensive about electricity and called the streetlights downtown "moonlight on a stick." Island-wide service was started in 1967. In 1970, MONLEC was formed by the government of Montserrat and the Commonwealth Development Corporation. Before then, electricity generation and distribution were managed by the Montserrat government through its public works department. By 1995, MONLEC had 5,600 customers.

In exchange for hosting the commemoration service in the Bethel Methodist Church, MONLEC installed the chandeliers which the church had earlier bought but couldn't afford to hang. (When we first went to the island, the church was illuminated by fluorescent tubes suspended from the vaulted ceiling.) The electric utility also strung lights in the yards of both the church and the manse next door. Those looked suspiciously like the Christmas lights that earlier were in downtown Plymouth. So maybe we wouldn't be allowed to keep them.

Margaret announced that we would wear all white for the MONLEC concert but no robes. I still didn't have a white skirt, which I told Paul Mabry and Margaret. At this, another choir member, named Claudia, said, "well, you have all day Friday and Saturday," meaning that surely I could whip up something by then. I supposed I would have to capitulate or not sing with them. But I was not thrilled about spending the money on something I'd perhaps wear only once.

As a newly minted champion of Plan B, I cut out a skirt from one of several white damask tablecloths we inherited with the house. It was worn and soft and stained in places but fortunately I was able to avoid the bad places or hide them in what would become the hem. From the church choir loft, no one would notice flaws or, even, what fabric my new skirt was made from.

At about 3:15 the day of the 4:30 p.m. MONLEC concert, we were driving past the church on our way home from Harris' when we realized people were already gathering. No one had told me I should be at the church an hour before the service was scheduled to start, but I saw choir members milling around just outside the church door. We rushed home so I could put on my new white skirt and an old white T-shirt, which had lacy trim, and I could walk up the hill to the church. By the time I arrived, it was 4 p.m., and the choir was already assembled, although the program wasn't to start for another half hour. All the seats in the church were full except for those reserved for dignitaries.

Billy's sister Mu-Mu forgot which collar she was supposed to wear with her robe and walked up the mountain to Tuitt's to retrieve the right one. But she arrived back in plenty of time. In fact, none of the choir members arrived after the concert started, a real surprise. And although some of them had taken music home, which was against Paul's rules, everyone returned his or hers. During the concert, I counted the new chandeliers, which were hung from high up on the beams of the steeply pitched ceiling. Already, I noted that seven of the candle-shaped light bulbs were burned out. A tall ladder, which I am not sure the church had, would be required to change a light bulb. I doubted that we could depend on MONLEC's driving all the way to the East to do that chore.

Immediately after the concert, we walked over to the manse, which was next door to the church, for the reception and to see the video of what we had just performed. The concert was exactly one hour long—by Paul's design. A lot of people seemed shocked that it didn't go on longer, and maybe even a little unhappy. We once heard a possibly apocryphal story—that a Montserratian woman complained to her minister, saying she had spent a long time getting ready for church, and she expected the service to last longer, making her time worthwhile.

Another concert was planned on short notice by the Anglican Church in Harris', and the Bethel Methodist Church was expected to take part. Nine choirs were to sing. Freddy Connor picked up quite a few of us in his van, including Marvella Eaton, who was new to the choir and who lived near the airport. She was waiting for Freddy by the Bethel rain shelter. Unfortunately, she had not realized we were to wear choir robes and hadn't brought hers, so Freddy drove her home to pick it up. All the way to Harris', she received a tongue-lashing from Margaret.

The church was already packed with people when we arrived, both choirs and the audience. The Anglican Church, like other buildings on the island, had no glass in the windows and no screens, so bats began flying in and zipping from one end of the sanctuary to the other, no more than three feet above the heads of the seated congregation. I could imagine the reaction a bat invasion would have on American women in similar circumstances, but the Montserratians were intent on the singing and paid no attention.

23
UPSET IN THE EAST

Rumors spread about plans for an expansion of the airport, which would affect Spanish Point, or parts thereof. Many people were worried about what was going to happen to their property. One rumor said that 20 houses would be torn down because the landing strip would be reoriented so as to avoid the need for planes to fly toward the cliff before turning to land. Another rumor had the runway extended but houses not affected. Still another said that just a few houses would be demolished.

Nancy told us that, for sure, money for the airport expansion had arrived from Britain. The British governor's wife, with whom she was friendly, had told her, she said. Right away, Nancy called the Montserratian chief minister to see if he knew what we could expect, and he promised to meet with the neighborhood "soon" to talk about the plans.

We learned that the trucks we all had been hearing down by the airport were only people removing sand from the beach near the runway to use in the making of concrete, which they weren't supposed to do. It wasn't earth-moving equipment getting ready to demolish part of Spanish Point, as had been rumored.

True to his word, Rupert McMillan, the chief minister, set up a meeting with the neighbors of Spanish Point to talk about the airport expansion. About 15 of us gathered on the Stewarts' pool deck to hear him talk and were disappointed that we didn't learn anything we didn't already know. A study had been done, he said. The UK and the European Union had committed funds to the project. The chief minister said there were two possible configurations: extending the existing runway, slanting it a bit more inland than it was previously, or slanting it inland quite a bit more than it was at the moment.

Yes, yes, we knew all that. And what we knew, or didn't know, was what was getting the neighbors upset. Whichever plan was chosen wouldn't be decided, McMillan said, until it was "costed out" the following May or June. That would be in 1995. There was another consideration, which hadn't received much attention from anybody: Amerindian artifacts had been found near the existing airport. And archeologists had been coming to the island to dig. In fact, since the 1970's, waves of scientists had been studying the Indian encampment. The Amerindians were thought to have had quite a sophisticated civilization on the island from 500 BC until about 500 AD.

Scientists had stepped up their digging because the site was in the middle of where the Montserrat government wanted to build the terminal for the new airport. The goal of the present expedition was to mark the boundaries of the site, so the government would at least know what was underground. An archaeologist had shown our friends Melvin and Nancy Stewart a skeleton they recently had found. Carlton, Nancy said, had been hanging around to watch the dig, too. In years past, before his brain was quite so fried, she thought he might even have helped the archaeologists with their work.

It could be, we thought, that nothing would happen concerning the airport expansion, mainly because there were several pieces to the funding package, and each was dependent upon the others. Perhaps it was wishful thinking, but my prediction was that they would spend so much money on studies they wouldn't be able to afford the more ambitious plan to shift the runway a great deal inland. If my suspicions were correct, we didn't have to worry about our house being destroyed.

McMillan talked at the meeting as if the owners of the doomed houses would know by June, and they would have to vacate by December, 1995, so that construction could begin in February of 1996. I said to myself, "No way would that happen."

With Spanish Point in turmoil over the airport, we barely noticed or made sense of unnatural phenomena that were occurring. One evening at 6:50 p.m. just before the Antigua news on TV, we felt the house throbbing and heard a chugging noise. Ed saw the window grates vibrating. Our first thought was that there had been a large explosion, but we concluded it was an earthquake. We realized this was the second biggest tremor we had felt since we arrived for the winter season of 1994. In truth, there had been swarms of small earthquakes that we had not felt.

Curious, we thought, and put the event out of our minds.

There were two more small earthquakes before church two days later. Each rumbled a bit, and the dishes rattled in the china cabinet. At church, Walter Lee told us there had been another quake at midnight on Friday, but we were asleep, apparently, and didn't feel or hear it. Later Sunday afternoon, William reported that a friend of his told him 10 tremors were felt in Plymouth over the period of a week. And the director of emergency preparedness on the island announced on Zed Jay Bee radio that seismic experts on Trinidad had been consulted.

The previous winter, we didn't feel any tremors. What was happening? There were many more small earthquakes during the winter season of 1994-1995, but we became used to them or didn't feel them at all. Going back up in 1995 was a sad occasion as we were traveling without our beloved Wishard and Sunny. Both had developed terrible bowel problems—the most delicate way to put it—and we reluctantly decided to put them down. Wishard, a Labrador Retriever, was 14 years old, and his companion, Sunny, was 16.

Over the summer, we grieved, although we knew we had done the right thing. While shedding many a tear, we realized, at the same time, that we wouldn't have to hire more charter planes for the last leg of our journey to Montserrat. And we wouldn't have to bribe the vet on Antigua.

In early August, we were in London at the end of a month-long driving vacation in England and Scotland when the owner of the B&B in which we were staying gave us a small article clipped from the newspaper. It was a Reuters story, saying that 1,000 people had been evacuated from the Chances Peak area of Montserrat because of a possible volcanic eruption. Rupert McMillan, the chief minister, was quoted as saying scientists had told him there was no danger to Plymouth, the capital.

Volcanic eruption? What? Could this really be happening? It seemed surreal. Ed immediately called Evelyn Sweeney, who had a home in London, to find out if she knew anything. She said she had learned through a phone call the day before that everyone had been evacuated from Long Ground, Tuitt's, Bethel, Bramble and Spanish Point and that 11 steam vents had been found on the Eastside. One, she said, was right up the hill from our neighborhood. Cinders had been falling on cars throughout the area, Evelyn said.

When we returned to Indianapolis from our English trip, we learned through a friend who searched via his Internet connection that the volcanic activity was about three miles southwest of our house and up on the side of Castle Peak, which was directly above the village of Long Ground. The vent there was belching dust and sulfur dioxide, as much as 1,000 tons a day.

Ed learned from an amateur radio friend living on Montserrat's Westside that in fact residents of the East had been evacuated for a week. A government public information officer had been named to update residents every day. The "ham," as amateur radio enthusiasts are called, and Ed made arrangements to attempt a contact Tuesdays and Fridays at 5 p.m. The next day, we had a call from another Montserrat property owner, who said the soufriere blew the day before, spewing volcanic ash 8,000 feet into the air. The ash was so thick in Plymouth that the streetlights came on.

Nevertheless, we still believed that the burbling of the soufriere would keep the pressure from building up, as we had been reassured all along. Despite the optimism we tried to feel, there was a niggling thought that perhaps our Paradise East was in for some hard times.

On August 22 of that year, there had been a rather large blow from an Eastside vent of the volcano, and the whole south end of the island had been evacuated, not just the villages of the East. Television news carried a small story, which reported that "an upscale tourist destination" was undergoing volcanic activity. Upscale? I thought about all the goats and cows that were tethered—or not—in my neighborhood and all the hours without water because of burst pipes, and I was amused.

August 24, in the year 79 AD, Pompeii was destroyed by the eruption of Mt. Vesuvius. And this was August, almost the 24th.

We learned that the HMS *Southampton*, a British ship, was cruising off-shore from Montserrat waiting for mass evacuations should they be necessary, and the island's governor, who lived in the historic Government House mansion on the mountain slope just to the south of Plymouth, had moved to a large estate on the Northwest Side. Presumably, that was in a safe area. Plymouth, the center of commerce, was abandoned. No one knew for how long.

I couldn't just sit and worry. So I went to the library in Indianapolis to see what I could learn about Montserrat's volcanic history. The last eruption on our little island was in 1632, according to one book I skimmed. Other islands in the region had a much more active history. Martinique, for example, had had 53 eruptions, the last of which was in 1932. The most notable of these eruptions, however, was in 1902 with 30,000 killed when Mt. Pelee erupted. Because of mass evacuations in recent times, there had been no fatalities in the Caribbean linked to volcanic activity.

On Wednesday, August 30, 1995, our Spanish Point neighbor, Nancy Stewart, called from the island to say she and her husband had moved temporarily to the Westside of the island. They obtained a pass and drove to Plymouth to buy food, she said, from the tailgates of trucks operated by Ram's and Angelo's supermarkets. The most distressing news she had to tell us was that Vic and Gladys Henry had fled to Antigua and put their house on the market. They wouldn't be coming back according to Nancy. Vic had been paying our bills when we weren't on island and overseeing the cutting of our grass. We guessed all that would stop and we would have to make other arrangements.

As if the volcano wasn't enough, hurricane Luis with winds of 140 miles an hour bore down on the island the first part of September, but it did its major damage on Antigua. Montserrat suffered from wind and lots of rain, however. Nancy and Melvin, who had gone back to their Spanish Point home, weathered Luis huddled in their bedroom for hours without electricity. When electricity was restored, they learned from the radio that roof damage on the island was severe. They would go out the next day to check on our house, Nancy said.

Whether from hubris or ignorance, or some of both, we continued to plan on returning to Montserrat in November. Surely that volcanic nonsense would be over by then, we thought. Right along, we had been buying things to take down: athletic shoes (called "trainers" by Montserratians) for Nicole's daughters, new burners for the Stewarts' gas stove, a food processor, and glazes for the pottery we expected to be making.

Our plane tickets were for November 28. Flying over the island, we tried to see the volcano, or where we thought it was, but the sky was overcast and foggy. The news wasn't good, we discovered after we landed. The town of Long Ground was to be evacuated that very night. Scientists from several countries, who had taken up residence on the island and were monitoring the volcano, were afraid that a lava dome might be growing under some thick fog. The first report we heard on Zed Jay Bee said Long Ground residents were to go to the Bethel School for their safety.

Wilma, the Canadian woman who had moved in next door, came over to show us where in the mountain range behind our house the volcano was located. She told us there were at least two active vents, one to the southwest just above the Tar River Estate, the ruin of which we could see from our backyard. There, ash mixed with water had caused mudslides in some of the ghauts. She thought the other vent was in a crater atop Chance's Peak, the highest spot on the island and immediately behind our house to the west.

The clouds lifted somewhat, and one thing was for sure; the mountains' outlines didn't look the same as they did when we left in the spring. Partly, Wilma said, that was because the toxic gases had killed the foliage, and the rock was exposed. Scientists would be trying to fly over the vents in a helicopter sometime that day.

We continued to believe that the crisis would soon be over. Through Cable and Wireless (the telephone company), we now had the capability of hooking up to the Internet, so we could send e-mails to our children. And an ATM machine had been installed outside the Royal Bank of Canada. The island was moving into the modern age —just a bit behind.

On Monday, December 1, Wilma gave Ed and me a booklet of evacuation plans—from a "Phase 1" evacuation of Long Ground to a full "red alert" evacuation of the entire island. The night before, we had packed small suitcases with important papers, our medicines and some clothing and hoped we wouldn't have to use them. Our evacuation booklet said that, should the entire island need to be evacuated, it would be done through the beaches on the Westside and Northside of the island. How that could be done I wasn't sure, as the road was narrow and had a scary series of hairpin turns. One of our friends bought himself a rubber raft in which he intended to escape. I was sure the surf would immediately turn it over and toss him out.

24

EVACUATION

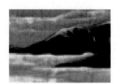

Some people were cocksure, as we were, that the volcano would soon wind down, and we would be able to get on with our lives. Others, however, listened to those in the know, or supposedly in the know. William warned us he had heard the East would be evacuated at 8 p.m. that very night.

We had filled our pool about 1/4 full and had purchased a refrigerator full of food. And we were somewhat shocked to learn from the radio that what William had heard was true: the Eastside of the island from the airport south, including us, and the southern villages on the island's Westside, were to be evacuated by 8 p.m. Scientists, said the announcer, were concerned about recent volcanic activity, including a gradual increase in the size of the lava dome in "English's Crater." That was part of the mountain complex listed on a map of the island as the "Soufriere Hills."

We were to take clothing and our medicines and go to our "shelter spot." The "eastern corridor," including the town of Plymouth, was in the evacuation zone. This meant that stores and the banks would have to be relocated to the North of the island. We packed our clothes and the food we had just purchased, our electronic equipment, our tax papers, checkbook, passports, books to read, cameras and all the glazes I had bought for pottery making, assuming that French's Studio was in the safe zone. We also turned off the water and gas, thinking we might be gone for a while.

Wilma refused to move. Our friends the Stewarts planned to go to the home of a friend on the Westside. We headed toward the home of new friends in the West, where we had been promised a place to stay.

In the North and West, life proceeded as it always had. You hardly noticed that you shared the island with a volcano. Many announcements on the radio were worth paying attention to. Osborne's Grocery, which had been located in the heart of Plymouth, was being moved to a room at the Vue Pointe Hotel, which also was owned by the Osborne family. Francine Collins, our hairdresser, planned to operate out of her home in Olveston, another subdivision on the Westside. We began making a list of which businesses were where.

According to radio reports, the authorities believed the relocation period might be three or four weeks. Ed and I had decided what we would do if the evacuation did indeed go on that long. We could either go back to Indianapolis or rent a place in the safe zone of the island. We decided that, after a week with our friends, we would reassess our position. It was a very unsettling and unsettled time.

At least, we didn't have to stay in a public shelter. People who lived in Plymouth were to be housed in the Anglican Church in Salem, the Salem Seventh-day Adventist Church and the Salem Church of God of Prophecy. The holiness church in Salem had agreed to take only members of the holiness church in Plymouth. According to a Zed Jay Bee report, there would be no food rations provided in the shelters until Sunday, one day hence, so people were asked to take plenty of food with them and to share with others. There was a Red Cross on the island, but it apparently wasn't set up to provide meals for hungry evacuees. Lucy's house was in the area to be evacuated, so there would be no Meals on Wheels.

From Zed Jay Bee, we learned that the hospital had moved to a school in St. John's, a town in the North, and that the Royal Bank of Canada would reopen in "Steadroy Riley's garage in Olveston." The cable TV office relocated, according to the radio, "two houses down from Dr. Allison's on Bishop's View Road." With directions like those, only people in the know would be able to find the relocated businesses. Family Life Services announced it was operating a mobile contraceptive service truck.

Our friend Tony James, the ham radio expert on the island, had already suffered tragedies related to the volcano. His wife Elba was killed in a terrible auto accident at the time of the first evacuation in the summer, and he was badly hurt. Apparently, many bones on his right side: hip, thigh, knee, shin and ankle were broken, and doctors told him he might not walk again. But he was getting around with crutches and had just returned to the island after a month in England for physical therapy.

Because of his injuries, the most he could do was sit around. But people who were not injured were doing the same thing. We saw them sitting, just sitting, on steps, walls and lawn of the Salem school and outside the bars. They were waiting, for what they did not know.

According to the volcano report on the radio, there was growth in the vent that had opened up on July 18—the one Medford had written about in a letter to us—and a "spine" of hardened, molten material had been extruded. Scientists feared this spine would break off and rocks would roll down the Tar River, which was very near Long Ground. The scientists also feared that lava would spill out and flow down the west side of the mountain toward Plymouth.

My list of what businesses had moved and to where they had moved was growing. Customs, for example, was relocated to the subdivision of Old Towne "next door to Leo Herbert's," according to a report on the radio. The treasurer's office was "just beyond Carmen French's." The Emerald Café and the Floss Snackette were "hanging out above the day care center in St. John's."

On December 6, the BBC's "Caribbean Report" said officials were extremely worried about 60- and 70-year-olds still living in Long Ground, Bethel and Spanish Point and refusing to move. That included some of our friends.

As if we didn't have enough trouble, there were at least two confirmed cases of dengue fever, so the health ministry announced it would begin mosquito fogging. Salem, near where we were staying, was to be treated daily from 5:30 -7:30 a.m. and from 5:30-7:30 p.m. We were being asked to leave our windows open during that time, presumably so mosquitoes could be killed inside homes, there being no screens on most windows. This was, to me, like asking to be poisoned. No one said anything about covering food and protecting pets, and both spray times were when a house's occupants were likely to be eating.

According to a representative of the tourist board, trying to put a happy face on things, the volcano had put Montserrat on the map. Two tour boats had come in since the evacuation, and 10 more were expected in the next three or four weeks.

We hadn't figured out where to pick up our mail. When we checked at the Salem Post Office, where most of the island's mail had been taken, we were told they didn't know where Bethel mail was and suggested we call the "media center." That was sort of the catch-all place for information. No one at the media center knew, but suggested Ed call the Salem Post Office later in the day. He did, and no one answered the phone.

The Delta gas station at the corner of Cork Hill Road and Lover's Lane in the Plymouth area had been opened to the public, and the police barricade moved to just beyond the gas station's driveway. This was an expedient way to avoid complaints, as the only other source of gas now that Rondo's in the East was evacuated was the Texaco station "up north." We later learned that government vehicles and essential workers' vehicles were being serviced at the Texaco station on Church Road, in downtown Plymouth, but only with a pass.

On December 8, we set off for Spanish Point via the North Road to check on our house. A checkpoint had been set up at the intersection of the road to the airport and the main road, and the policeman there wanted to know who we were and why we wanted to go into the evacuated area. Satisfied that we indeed lived in the area, he gave us a two-hour pass.

Our house looked fine except for the grass, which was about eight inches tall. The pool water, what there was of it, didn't look muddy or ashy, although it was full of leaves. Also, I noticed right away that a large, hairy spider—the kind I called "the Montserrat tarantula"—had taken up residence in the pool. Because we thought that in a few days or weeks we would be able to return home, Ed put chlorine tablets in the water to forestall the growth of algae. We picked up our computer printer, a few more clothes, some books, our first aid kit, and some fabric with which I planned to make some sort of wallhanging. We heard a helicopter flying in the area and looked outside to see "our" volcano with the helicopter doing aerial surveillance.

Back on the Westside, we queued up at the temporary facility of the Royal Bank of Canada, where a woman was selling barbeque chicken on the lawn. After cashing a check, we paid the water bill—in a house in the Woodlands subdivision, and we stopped at Suntex Bakery, where bread was being baked in a Hugo House.

The daily volcano reports seemed optimistic. One said "our" volcano could just grow a dome, for a few months or a few years, and never have a catastrophic eruption. One volcano in South America, the scientist spokesman said, had been growing a dome since the 1930s. He went through scenarios. The crater walls might collapse. Dome growth might be accompanied by small explosive "events." We might have a lava flow. Dome growth, he said, was a flow that got stuck. The Soufriere Hills were mostly made up of domes, but at some time along the way, one or more of the domes might have erupted. Then here was the kicker: Our current volcanic activity might actually have started in 1992 with a series of earthquake events. It became clear to us that scientists didn't know much more than we did—and that wasn't much.

By mid-December of 1995, Montserratians were getting restless. And so were some expats; one of them, our friend T.J., even petitioned the police chief to let us all go home. We were able-bodied, he said, and all of us had cars in which to make a quick escape. In the shelters, there had been cutlass duels, and someone had run down a policeman directing traffic.

The man who owned the house where some of our Spanish Point neighbors were staying died while sitting on the toilet. It took several people to remove the body from the bathroom as he was a large man. His widow was left to cope with the house, her houseguests and the volcano. Two earthquakes occurred overnight, one under the town of Windy Hill and one under the volcano

Paul arrived at our friends' house with a big package for us: 10 pounds of rice and 10 pounds of dry beans, a gift from the Bethel Methodist Church, the occasion being our evacuation. This was an embarrassment to us because we were living in relative luxury while others were sleeping on church pews, in tents or in overcrowded shelters with no privacy whatsoever. Paul said he had received some of this largesse himself and tried to give it all back, but the ladies of the church were adamant. He suggested that, if we gave the food away, we not tell from where it came.

A little late: The scientists who were on the island updated the residents on the volcanic activity on Montserrat for the past 100 years. They said there had been volcanic "incidents" every 30 years or so, a fact we had never known. These "incidents" never resulted in big eruptions, but there were swarms of small earthquakes and a few big ones. Even the vulcanologists said these incidents didn't amount to much—in contrast to what was currently happening.

In the 1996 book he edited, *Eruption: Montserrat and the Volcano,* Dr. Howard Fergus said it was taught in school that the last eruption of the Soufriere Hills volcano was 18,000-19,000 years ago. Although there may not have been people living on the island to report it, the volcano might actually have erupted violently as recently as 1630.

We were learning that what has become known as the "Wadge Report," named for one of its authors, Geoffrey Wadge, and titled "Volcanic Hazards from Soufriere Hills Volcano Montserrat" was published in 1987. Discussed in the Parliament of the United Kingdom, it outlined possible eruption scenarios. There is enough blame to go around in that the report was largely ignored in Britain, and some officials on Montserrat claimed that papers pertaining to it were lost in Hurricane Hugo. The paper predicted that at some point in the future Plymouth, particularly, might be adversely affected by volcanic activity and noted that new installations in the East and in the capital should not be constructed.

New installations were indeed constructed, and after Hurricane Hugo older buildings were rehabilitated in what became the unsafe zone. A prime example was Glendon Hospital, which was badly damaged in the hurricane, was almost completely rebuilt and then could never be used because of the Soufriere Hills eruptions. A concluding and chilling paragraph in the report, written eight years before the first violent activity in 1995, said "Soufriere Hills Volcano is active and will erupt again. It is a potential threat to many of the people that live in southern Montserrat." Somehow the words "who knew?" took on real significance in our suddenly dangerous scenario.

25
LIVING WITH DANGER

The scientists who had come to the island from all over the world to monitor the volcano's activity beginning with the first steam eruptions in 1995 said that after a lull in activity, there would be a "phased stand-down" before people would be allowed to go back home. I thought this was so much government blah-blah. There had been 20 earthquakes in the past 24 hours. One measured 3.0 on the Richter scale. The scientists couldn't afford to make a mistake or innocent people might be killed.

On December 18, police found a body in Harris', an elderly man who had refused to evacuate as he'd been asked. The public was asked to report any elderly person known to be living in the unsafe zone. But perhaps the public didn't know. The man might have died in normal times, too, but his death, alone in an abandoned village, was creepy and sad. By the next day, scientists said a number of glowing rocks were visible in the crater, and a large glowing crack was seen during a helicopter fly-over. This meant that the domes were still growing, in a cluster, coalescing into one.

Stray dogs were killing livestock in the unsafe zone, said the announcer on Zed Jay Bee. Apparently, farmers simply cut loose cows, goats and sheep and left them behind when they went to the shelters. These animals were eating crops left growing in farmers' fields. Perhaps vengeful farmers were the ones who turned the dogs loose. Supposedly $30,000 worth of livestock had been destroyed.

The governor spoke on the radio, announcing that we would not be allowed to go to our homes until after Christmas at least. Then the scientists would make an assessment. We were wearing out our welcome at our friends' house, as the waiting wore on us all. So we started looking for a place to rent in the West. Sixty-one persons, according to a radio report, had chosen to stay in their homes in the unsafe zone. Another man was found dead, this time in Molyneaux. He also was elderly.

The next day, a realtor took us to see a house in Fox's Bay that had been empty three years, but was being painted and could be rented for $750 US a month. There was furniture we could use, but it was of '50s vintage and pretty banged up. There were bugs in all the kitchen drawers. The windows didn't fit, and mosquitoes and thieves would have easy access. The sheets in the closets had been stored in plastic bags and probably were full of cockroaches. Trash littered the floors.

We looked at several more houses in various states of coming apart at the seams, but then the real estate agent said she had found a house, two bedrooms and a pool, that she thought we might like. The house was owned by a young woman who had gotten a divorce and gone back to the States. We learned later she had defaulted on her mortgage, so the bank owned it. We would be charged $750 a month if we would agree to take care of swimming pool maintenance.

We had not seen the inside of the house, but said yes to the terms of the rental anyway. Moving day could be almost immediately. Christmas was approaching, and several Spanish Pointers were determined to go to their homes and cook Christmas dinner there, never mind the volcano. We decided to pass on that. But we did try to get into the holiday spirit by taking part in as many activities in the safe zone as we could, such as the choir party at Paul and Adele's house.

We were singing carols around the Mabrys' keyboard when the mosquito foggers arrived. They didn't stay out in the streets, as we expected, but entered yards and walked around houses spraying as they went, never mind the fact that the windows were open. The fog billowed into the house in great clouds, making it impossible to see from one side of the living room to the other. I have wondered ever since what the long-term effects of this might be.

Despite the unknown state of the volcano, we were allowed to go back to Spanish Point for two hours so we could cut the grass. Our neighbor William also was there, he said, to slaughter a goat, part of which he wanted to share with us. We told him we would take a raincheck until we were settled in our rental and suggested that he might want to think about giving whatever he couldn't eat himself to someone who didn't have any meat for Christmas dinner.

William had never talked about his first recent knowledge of the volcano, but in a reminiscing mood, he said he was up on the mountain above Tuitt's on July 18, 1995 when "she blew" for the first time. There was a great roaring noise, which William at first thought was a truck motor. But then the roaring got louder, and soon there were rocks being hurled up in the air. "I ran because I was scared," William said. "You should have seen that, mon."

After I ate my peanut butter sandwich, and Ed had a can of sardines, we hurried toward the West with William in the back seat. He said he had fully intended to start walking up the North Road when he was finished tending his animals, less the one he butchered, and hoped someone would come along to pick him up. He was living temporarily down a very narrow road that hugged a cliff with no guard rails, a steep drop-off and hardly enough room for two cars to pass. On the other side of that road were several one-room bars, and what made the traffic all the more hair-raising was that several elderly, drunken men staggered up and down along that road. William's mother, age 93 by this time, had been taken to the island's old folks' home, which was located on another nail-biter of a road farther north.

This was our Christmas Eve. By Christmas Day, there were huge changes in the volcano. A large spine had been extruded, much like toothpaste from a tube, over two days. And there was some danger of its collapsing. There were three earthquakes Sunday, meaning that magma was moving underground. Still, we were allowed into our house in Spanish Point, where Ed and I exchanged gifts and sat on the porch, gazing out at the ocean and Antigua. It was a sad day, far away from family and friends, facing an uncertain future on the island we loved so much.

Later in the day, we obtained the key to our rental house and were able to see inside for the first time. There were dead cockroaches all over—on the floors and in the drawers in the kitchen—but we would clean them up, just as we had cleaned them up in the Spanish Point house. At least the exterminators had done their work. Otherwise, what we saw was great: two bedrooms, two baths with showers, a living/dining room, kitchen and a 30-foot swimming pool. In addition, the house had a roofed outdoor room with wicker furniture plus a white plastic table and chairs. We couldn't wait to get started making a temporary home there.

When Ed went to sign the rental agreement, the realtor removed the paragraph which said the tenant, when vacating the premises, must return the property in the same shape he/she found it. "I don't want you collecting and strewing dead bugs around," she said.

The days following were full of shopping, bill paying and other errands, made more difficult by the fact that places of business had mostly been moved, and we learned their locations from the Zed Jay Bee or word of mouth. Ed had a flat tire, which the two men who helped him change it said was caused by dry rot. We had bought two tires the year before, but the others hadn't been replaced in seven years. Ed found out who had tires to sell, but when he went there, the business was closed as it was Wednesday afternoon. He was able to get a pass to drive in to the Texaco station in Plymouth, where he bought two new tires. The two he didn't replace had nails in them, so he had those repaired. When he returned "home," Ed reported that Plymouth was a ghost town except for some mangy dogs.

Scientists admitted that before the evacuation they feared there would be pyroclastic flows in the East and a 5 percent chance of a major eruption. But since then, the activity had changed. Spines had collapsed, but areas near the crater were still dangerous because of toxic gases, hot rocks and acid rain. (Pyroclastic flows, made of hot gases and rocks, travel at 100 MPH. Mount St. Helens produced a giant pyroclastic flow when it erupted in May of 1980.)

In addition, sophisticated monitoring devices had been set up, allowing islanders to be warned of an impending catastrophic eruption 24 hours before it happened. The governor announced on the radio that if the level of activity stayed the same, "a phased return to selected areas might be possible." But, he continued, some parts of the island might be too dangerous to inhabit.

Although the governor's speech was much anticipated, we didn't know what it meant for the people living in the East. Our rental period was one month, so if the authorities were to send us home in two weeks—or send us home and then evacuate us again—we would have a place to go, a comforting thought. But if not? Being a couple of stateless people would be very stressful.

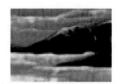

26
DECISIONS

We were not kept in the dark for long. Within a few days, on about January 1, 1996, the British governor came on the radio at 6:30 a.m. to announce that Montserratians could go back to their homes and businesses, as the scientists said that, for the present at least, the volcano posed no threat. The order, however, did not apply to Long Ground, Spanish Point, Bramble Village and Tuitt's. Our situation would be reassessed in mid-January. He said the decision was being made on purely scientific grounds, not on economic or political grounds, as had been rumored. He said there was still danger from ash surges and avalanches in the towns to which residents were not being allowed to return. To keep people out of the "unsafe zone," the police would block off the entrance to Spanish Point, but you could apply for passes at the Bethel Methodist Church.

Big news: Shops were closing down in their temporary quarters in the North of the island and preparing to move back to Plymouth, where grass was growing up in the street by this time. Day by day, restless people were appearing in town, as if awakening from a long snooze. When we stopped off at the post office in town to pick up our mail, where Ed had heard it was, the woman behind the counter said that for some reason Bethel's mail had been held in Antigua. We would get it eventually, she said. The woman also said Mrs. Myers was quite ill and that even after we returned to Spanish Point, someone else would have to take over the Bethel post office duties.

The next day, the early-morning announcer on Zed Jay Bee said Christmas mail was finally coming in. The official line was that it was held up because of a government shut-down in the US, but we had heard that a bunch of it had been found over in Antigua, stacked in an out-of-the-way corner. We returned to the post office at about 12:30 p.m. to ask about our mail, but were told to come back at 1 p.m.

When we returned, another woman gave us a fat stack of Christmas cards and a notice that customs had a package for us. For a change, we were able to "spring" this package with no distress at all.

The day of the assessment of the volcano situation finally arrived. In anticipation of being allowed back home to Spanish Point at last, we drove over to ready the house for occupancy. On the way, near Katy's house, we were met by Brandon Timmons, who lived in a Hugo House with a good view of the volcano. "Did you see the fire on the mountain Sunday night," he wondered? Brandon said the dome glowed red until 11 p.m.

We decided to make the big move back to the East the next day. It would be a bittersweet return as we had only slept in our little house two nights since we had returned to the island the end of November. It was January 15 when the "all clear" was sounded, with the proviso that we might have to be evacuated again if the volcano started acting up once more.

During a Zed Jay Bee speech shortly after "the day of return," the governor said 200 people had refused to leave their homes during the evacuation, putting police and health care workers at risk. But he said he understood many people were very suspicious of the government, as the volcano kept ramping up and then quieting down. People didn't like having their lives disrupted, and they wondered if the government were crying wolf. But, he emphasized, the government was doing the best it could, using the scientific data from the MVO (Montserrat Volcano Observatory.) Although the scientists couldn't predict exactly what was going to happen in the future, they did know what happened at the soufriere in the 1930s and the 1960s, the governor went on. Then, there were increasing numbers of earthquakes, but no catastrophic eruptions, for up to two years. "This round of activity might follow a similar pattern," he said.

One evening, the head of the Montserrat Volcano Observatory, Dr. Waldron Forest, spoke on the radio about historical and recent events surrounding the volcano. Caribbean islands from Grenada near South America to Saba near the Virgin Islands are volcanic, he said, but Antigua and Anguilla stopped seismic activity about 25 million years before. What we called the "Soufriere Hills" was really five domes, and until the current awakening of the volcano, there had been three volcanic crises in the past 100 years.

1897-98—strong earthquakes, causing damage to structures. Increased gases came out of the island's already existing soufrieres.

1930s—much damage to churches and estate buildings due to earthquakes. One of the soufriere areas showed increased gas emission, and a scientist was nearly suffocated by the gas.

1966-67—There were many earthquakes, the maximum of which was a 4.0 on the Richter scale. Certainly nobody had told us about volcanic and seismic activity on the island in the past, and it seemed to us that most Montserratians were unaware there might be problems. Some older people were aware, however, especially when reminded that, yes, there were groups of earthquakes at certain periods in the past, and some people were afraid to live in their homes.

1992-1995—There were 18 periods of increased earthquakes, the largest being in November and December, 1994. All of these, Dr. Forest said, may have been part of the pattern that started way back in 1897.

Geologic research had shown there was a big eruption in 1632, and scientists knew that one included a pyroclastic flow, Dr. Forest noted.

How safe were we, really? Leave the island? Not at this point. After all, our home, the beautiful and meaningful home we had invested so much in, was here and we were reluctant, very reluctant, to leave it. Besides, the "authorities" weren't really warning us of anything continuingly dire.

After we relocated to Spanish Point, Margaret phoned to say we should come to the Methodist manse to pick up some emergency food. Ed told her we had already received our portion while we were staying in the West. He felt embarrassed to be receiving that bag, much less more gifts from a relief organization in the United States. Since we were members of the church, Margaret said, we were supposed to be receiving this second shipment. She would not be dissuaded.

We drove up to the manse at 4 in the afternoon, and there were Margaret and another church member, ready to pass out our relief supplies: 10 pounds of dry kidney beans, 2 cans of Pam, 5 pounds of rice, 3 boxes of raspberry Pop Tarts and a big box of Crispix cereal.

That evening after dark, Ed and I went outside to see if we could spot the glow Brandon Timmons and some of our neighbors were talking about. Oh, yes, they weren't kidding. There was an all-over, low-level glow, and then, at times, there would be flashes of bright material, such as happens when charcoal briquets in a backyard grill catch fire. Using binoculars, I could even see glowing boulders tumbling down the mountainside.

Because of the illness of Edith Myers, Sharon Jones took over as postmistress. There were a lot of changes in how the mail was distributed, and we had no choice but to be happy with her method. We surmised that Medford was alphabetizing the names on the pieces of mail before his mother returned from work at 5 p.m., for she almost immediately swung into postmistress mode, calling out the names beginning with the "A's."

This was a painfully slow way to do the job, but everybody stood silently and waited for their names to be called. As we learned the import of Sharon's distribution method, we altered how we dealt with our mail. We started driving up the hill instead of walking and going much later. By 5:40, when we arrived one day, dusk was closing in on her street clogged with cars and a long line. "Anton Morris, Tuitt's Village," we heard her say.

"Let's come back later," Ed said.

Although life was anything but normal, we somehow settled into our routine—even to driving Meals on Wheels. The first time, just after we had returned home, was special, with warm, but not hot, breezes, fluffy clouds and a blue sky, the kind of weather that would be rare in Indiana in winter.

In Cork Hill, a town north of Plymouth, we met a woman who helped Lucy by delivering food to five homes. She said she would no longer go to one old lady's home because "she cursed me." Lucy attempted to calm the helper down, saying the client was old and sick and that, without Meals on Wheels, she wouldn't have anything to eat.

But the helper was adamant. She would not serve food to anyone who cussed her out. So Lucy had us drive down a narrow, bumpy, rutted lane and stop outside while she went in and tried to reason with her unreasonable client, who was 90 and had stomach ulcers. Lucy told the woman that the volunteer bringing the food was doing a favor and didn't have to bring it. Returning Lucy and Elizabeth to their homes, we saw a loose pig eyeing a lamb, and Ed chased it away with a stick and threw a rock. The wild pigs, of which there were many on the island, were known to kill small warm-blood animals.

There was a growing kerfluffle in the neighborhood, too, making us feel that life was a little way back to normal, well, semi-normal. Knowing that we attended the Methodist church, one of our fellow snowbird neighbors called us to complain about the bells, which he insisted were ringing at 3 a.m. on Sunday mornings and waking up everybody on his block. Actually, I thought they had been ringing at 5 a.m. Sunday morning, which, I agreed, was a bit too early. He claimed that in years past the bells were rung at 6:30 a.m. on Sundays and then only 7 times. Now, he said, they were being rung 40 times. I told him that if he wanted to register a complaint, he should call Margaret Joseph, as she was the president of the congregation.

At choir practice the next day, Margaret said, "You sent that man to me" to complain about the bells. He phoned her on Sunday and then when the bells rang in the afternoon before the evening service, he walked up to the church and found her there. I told Margaret the bells rang at 5 a.m. on Sundays and woke people up. She said that was the point—that we should all get up and go to church. Apparently, she told the angry neighbor that the ringing of the bells had been going on for 100 years. The neighbor told her that he and his wife came to the island for peace and quiet.

I agreed with him. Besides, the bell ringing had gotten out of hand. Simon, the sexton, rang the bells 119 times on February 28 and then 84 times at 5:18 p.m. the next day. Margaret expressed disbelief. I told her I counted the peals myself. The upshot of all this was that the residents of Spanish Point got nowhere. For some of the white people, this had become a cause celebre. I was not into causes celebre. I just wanted to live at peace with my neighbors. But I fervently wished Simon would stop ringing the bells at 5 a.m. on Sunday mornings.

The truth is that I assumed that the volcano at some point would stop doing what it was doing so we could continue living in our home. Ever the optimist, I began peeling veneer from the dresser in our bedroom, ruined when it was drenched with rain water in Hurricane Hugo. After the veneer was peeled off, I aimed to sand and paint. The job required a putty knife and lots of elbow grease, as the veneer was loose in places and stuck tightly in others.

Back at the volcano, the dome was growing both vertically and horizontally. Several incandescent spots were noted by the scientists, according to the evening MVO report. Some of the southern part of the dome was falling apart, and stones had reached the upper Tar River area. As the dome grew, the amount of gas in the atmosphere was increasing. The haze we'd been seeing was "associated with sulfur dioxide," the MVO spokesman said. A mixture of this steam and the gases was causing what amounted to acid rain, which contained hydrochloric and sulfuric acids. But, he said, the amounts were not injurious to humans or animals in either the short or long-term. I wondered if that was true.

Ed awakened me one morning at 5:50 a.m. to see an exciting pyrotechnic display —much glowing on the volcano just before sunrise. I saw a red rock fall down the slope of the mountain close to the crater. Later on in the day, a scientist, giving the volcano report on the radio, said the increase in activity was not a cause for concern.

Meanwhile, the minister of the Bethel church said that for the past 7 1/2 months she had been saying God would see Montserrat through with the volcano, and that he was a merciful God. But, she said, she now believed that God's patience was wearing thin. Another Montserratian woman told me the volcanic eruptions were occurring because "Montserrat is a wicked society." What she meant by that I didn't know. Maybe too much sex or alcohol or both. Or too much rock and roll. Perhaps the minister had in mind the in-fighting within the choir over who was going to make decisions and who was going to lead. Alicia, a young girl in the choir, told me quietly that the enmities went back years. People should forget their differences and "in unity work for the glory of God," she said.

We bought primer and sandpaper, determined to go ahead with rehabilitating the poor old dresser and vanity in our bedroom. The wood was as soft as balsa, and I wondered how it would hold up. But it had survived—in battered condition—Hurricane Hugo. We had priced new dressers in the furniture stores on the island, and small, poorly made ones were priced at around $600 US.

I bought eight turquoise pulls for the dresser, forgetting I needed four more for the vanity. Luckily, Grimes' Wayside Store ordered some more for me, thus averting a problem. When I investigated buying the paint, I learned that most hardware stores were not able to mix custom colors. But I needed to match the turquoise drawer pulls I had bought from Grimes', and not just any paint would do. There is turquoise, and then there is turquoise: too blue, too green, too yellow. The clerk at Osborne's suggested we go either to Emerald Hardware or Darlington's, and we went to the latter to buy a gallon.

I asked for the resident paint mixer, and a very large Montserratian man with thick glasses said he was the one. I gave him the drawer pull I wanted him to match, and he asked me to wait for a bit as he had other customers. I had a chance to look around and discovered he had a paint mixing machine, with a lazy susan of "soda fountain" colors and a machine to shake up the mix. I was aghast, however, when I realized he had no recipes and no color charts. The mixer man had just a generic blue and yellow to work with. He squirted in some of this and some of that, and every now and then he held the drawer pull alongside what he had mixed up to see if they matched.

He fooled around so long trying to get the right color that the one-gallon can he started off with was no longer big enough to hold the paint. So he found a bigger can into which he poured the paint and added just a tad of orange to gray down the color. It ended up darker than I wanted, but it was the same general color of turquoise as the drawer pull, not too green, not too blue and not too yellow. Just right. Deciding not to push my luck, I didn't ask for another gallon of lighter turquoise. In the interest of covering up the dresser's many flaws, I had planned to paint a bottom coat of the darker turquoise and then apply a lighter coat which I would partly rub off so it would look marbleized. Instead, I bought some white paint with which to mix the top coat myself. As soon as we returned home, I started painting.

Ed's Meals on Wheels driving gave us no end of dinner-table conversation. The old man who used to hobble down from Long Ground to Tuitt's to receive his food could no longer walk. So Lucy began sending his food up on the school bus. She reported that Billy had taken his mother back to the old folks' shelter as she couldn't cope at home. The woman who sold vegetables across the street from Ram's berated Lucy about a woman she insisted needed to be taken to the old folks' shelter. No one was listening, she said.

It was a day for unpleasantness. A little old man in the town of Delvins, a village on the Westside of the island, said Lucy was trying to poison him, so she delivered his meal to a woman she knew in his village. This woman, as per agreement, would give it to another woman, who would take it up the hill to the man, but not until the car which brought Lucy was out of sight.

Some of the old people to whom we had been bringing food were either in the hospital or in the old folks' home in Cavalla Hill, a town in the North of the island. And this was a revolving situation. Lucy didn't know from week to week who her clients would be. Many recipients could be found sitting patiently, sometimes in the grass, sometimes at the side of the road, sometimes on their porches, waiting for their food.

Carlton told us he had gotten himself into trouble and had to appear in court. We learned later that he had gone to his mother to ask for food. The man who was then living with his mother refused, whereupon an argument ensued. Carlton hit or shoved, and the man fell down.

The first coat on the chest of drawers dried and looked beautiful. I mixed up some of the turquoise with white paint, the second coat. I had brought a piece of natural sponge from the States to do the daubing. Two days after that, when I was sure it was dry, I would put our clothes away.

On March 23, I was out in the backyard checking on one of our grapefruit trees when I looked up at the mountain just in time to see an amazing ash cloud come rolling down into the Tar River. Ed immediately called the Montserrat Volcano Observatory to report this information, which they were very glad to receive.

Unfortunately, the helicopter was on the fritz, so no scientist could come to investigate. Ash clouds continued for an hour or more, almost continuously, but the summit of the volcano was obscured by clouds. When those cleared away, we saw that one of the large spines was gone. We subsequently learned that the major ash cloud, at 8:23 a.m., dropped ash all over Plymouth.

The next Sunday, March 24, Simon rang the 6:30 a.m. bell only 25 times, but he made up for it at 8:45 when he rang it more than 500 times, by actual count. The neighbors who complained before certainly had plenty to complain about now. Despite the continuing volcanic activity, the scientists tried to allay our fears. And I continued to believe that the mountain was going to quiet down soon, even though it was currently having a temper tantrum.

I sanded the vanity in one morning; it was not going to be the horrible job the dresser had been. Mrs. Tolbert, the wife of our house's owner, had a bad infestation of cockroaches in the vanity, so I would have to paint drawers inside and out to cover up the cockroach poop stains. As ash clouds continued to billow up, and I continued to sand away, I couldn't help but think of the emperor Nero, who "fiddled while Rome burned."

On the radio, a scientist noted that the older the dome became the less likely it was that there would be an explosive eruption. The crater, which was U-shaped, was open to the East, toward us and Spanish Point. The absence of an eastern crater wall had always saved the Plymouth area in times past. "Dome failure to the East will likely again be the scenario," he said.

That didn't preclude pyroclastic flows and surges. The magnitude of threat wasn't yet large enough to warrant another evacuation, the scientist said, but one might be coming in the future. Things seemed so unstable and uncertain to us that we decided if another evacuation was called for, we would stay on the Westside for a week or however long it took to get our affairs in order and purchase tickets to fly back to Indianapolis.

The volcano's ash cloud shot 6,000 feet into the air one day, and children were told to wear masks to school to avoid breathing the ash. Schools in Plymouth were closed for the day, and many shops closed early, too. Within two days after that, I heard what sounded like thunder and looked up at the mountain in time to see rocks rolling down and a huge ash cloud rising several thousand feet in the air. From there, it was borne on the trade winds toward Plymouth. The head of the MVO faxed Zed Jay Bee, the radio station, with the statement: "There is no cause for alarm."

I painted the first coat on the vanity and let it dry. While I was putting the final sponge coat on, we received a phone call. "You're kidding," Ed said. I knew exactly what had happened: The prospective buyers of our Indianapolis home had accepted our counter offer. But there was kind of a hitch: they wanted possession 30 days after closing, which was scheduled for April 29. This meant we'd have to scramble to move out of the house, and we weren't even back there yet. Still, we'd been trying to sell the historic house, located in downtown Indianapolis, for three years, so it behooved us to hustle.

It was then April 3. Ed immediately called a friend who lived in the Indianapolis apartment complex where we wanted to rent and asked if she would sign us up. It was time to go. And the pieces were fitting together. Friends from the Westside of Montserrat, who would soon return to Canada for the summer, offered their house for two to three days in case of another evacuation. They had heard Long Ground was going to be evacuated that very day. Zed Jay Bee confirmed that news. Residents in Long Ground were to be relocated for the nighttime hours until the collapsing dome situation was not so critical. They could go to the old school behind the Bethel church, the report said.

The minister of health said, "Be patient and trust in God. This administration will always move on the side of caution." Hot rock avalanches had reached as far as the Tar River Valley. This meant the devastation was inching down the mountain right toward our house. In town that morning, we went looking for dust masks. The first store I tried didn't have any, but as we drove up another street, we saw two kinds taped to the door of the video store. So Ed hurriedly parked the car, ran in and bought two of those plus a package of fat-free strawberry cookies.

At 2:30 p.m. that day, we received the official word: we had to be out of our home by evening.

What to do. We had the "going home" half of our round-trip tickets to Indianapolis, but they weren't for a return until May. Renters were living in our house in Indianapolis, and we hadn't yet told them they would have to leave soon because of the impending sale. Now it seemed we needed the house ourselves. There was only one solution. We needed to exchange our airline tickets for an earlier departure as soon as possible and find a place to stay on Montserrat temporarily until we could fly.

Friends living in Fox's Bay agreed to take us in, although they were suffering from falling ash themselves, and their guest bedroom was being used for storage. We said we didn't care, that we would help them clean up the ash and move what was on the bed so we could sleep there. Ed called our travel agent and arranged to have the airline tickets moved up. In a few minutes, she called back to say she was unable to find a booking until the 10th of April, a week away.

As calmly as possible, we started packing, using a "bug-out list" we had prepared earlier, just in case. Meanwhile, clouds of ash rolled down the mountain, ever closer to us. I didn't care what the scientists said a couple of days before; I thought we were in extreme danger.

I was outside in the backyard when a particularly strong pulse sent hot ash rushing down the mountain. The surge set some trees on fire in the Tar River Valley just south of Long Ground, the place where we had met T.J.'s wife in their pick-up truck after our hike. I'm not usually prone to colorful language, but I yelled, "What the f--- are we doing here?" It was about 3 p.m. The ash obliterated the sun as it blew out to sea toward Antigua. Blue smoke borne on the wind from the burning trees mixed with the ash and assaulted our nostrils as we hurriedly loaded the car with some of our clothes and the wall hanging I'd been quilting. Ed locked the doors, turned off the gas and shut off the water and electricity, the same as he always did when we were getting ready to go back to the States in the spring.

At the Fox's Bay house of our friends, everything was covered with a gray dust, including all the plants, the cars, the sidewalks, the grass and, inside, all the furniture despite keeping the windows closed. Ed and our host washed cars, vacuumed walkways and hosed off plants, which would have died otherwise. I helped our hostess brush ash off the porch screens and integrate the food we'd brought into her already bulging refrigerator.

The scientist's report that night, in contrast to the reassurance of earlier, included what would happen if you were caught in a pyroclastic flow. Those in the direct path would be fried. Those on the periphery would have their brains boiled in their skulls. And farther away, people would be burned severely. Obviously, the purpose of this report was to scare Montserratians into evacuating to the safe zone.

On April 5, the early-morning volcano update said residents could go into the unsafe zone without a pass in order to pick up household goods they weren't able to grab when the evacuation began. So immediately after breakfast, we left our friends' house for Paradise East, carrying lists of things to do. We were instructed to leave radios on so we could listen to Zed Jay Bee in case volcanic activity increased dangerously while we were in our homes. My major job was to package up and seal all the rice and dried beans we'd been given as relief supplies and to take away all the rest of the food we'd left behind in the cupboards. I wiped out the refrigerator and planted the philodendron I'd been rooting. I also picked two grapefruit and told our trees goodbye, until the fall, or so I told myself.

There's nothing to speed up work like fear; we were finished with our chores in half an hour. Just as we drove over to the Stewarts' to tell them goodbye and give them our house keys, "Amazing Grace" was playing on the radio.

On Sunday of that week, the Mabrys were to fly back to Canada; we had arranged to take them to the airport and afterwards move into their house for Sunday night, Monday and Tuesday, which was our day to fly.

When we arrived at the Mabrys,' Paul was still wearing his

bathing suit because he didn't want to go. But Adele made him get dressed so we could start off for the airport, a 45-minute drive when there was no traffic. There was sure to be a lot of traffic now that everyone had moved to the North of the island, she said. That turned out to be true. People were wandering around, rootless and worried. People like a man called "Mocha," who always called Ed "Poppy," I guess because of his gray beard. People like Tony James, who had driven to the Eastside of the island just to see a huge spine, taller than the highest mountain on the island. It was shaped like a witch's hat, originally standing straight up, but now listing to the left. At the airport, we saw neighbors from Spanish Point who were defying the authorities and remaining in their homes.

People who stayed in the unsafe zone were "outed" on the radio as soon as they were discovered. "Cynthiana Thomas in Windy Hill, we ask you to walk out to the main road, and the Montserrat Defense Force will pick you up," the announcer said. In another case, the announcer said that a girl, her two children and her boyfriend were still in Harris'. "We ask you to consider your children," he said.

Maybe the people still in Spanish Point would hear this and evacuate as they were asked to, but I doubted it as many expats did not listen to the local radio station. We were able to see a film of the pyroclastic flow taken on April 3, the event which caused us to flee. It was quite spectacular and showed the extent of the burning and the ecological disaster that was caused. I think it was then that we really realized how vulnerable our house was. We might never see it again.

Scientists were beginning to talk about the possibility of "the Big One." That might mean an explosion with a column of hot ash and gases rising straight up from the main vent. As the column collapsed, the material might come down the flanks of the volcano at breakneck speed. Something similar happened about 26,000 years before, they reported.

The Montserratian government was toying with the idea of purchasing sheep and goats from farms in Long Ground and Bethel as a means of keeping farmers from going into the dangerous East to care for their animals. Whether that meant the government would round up the animals and slaughter them or let them die and compensate the farmers, no one seemed to know or would say.

The day for us to fly back to the States arrived, after sleepless nights. I worried that the volcano might blow its top and keep us from leaving, maybe killing us as we boarded the plane. Ed was more pragmatic; he thought about the possibility of ash being sucked up in the plane's engines. The airport was just at the edge of the unsafe zone, and we could stand on the sidewalk outside the terminal and look up at the dome growing about 3 1/2 miles away. We could also see our subdivision in the distance, but couldn't pick out our house as it was obscured by trees.

Yvette Oliver, who lived in Long Ground and had been relocated to the Judy Piece Methodist Church, asked me, "Mrs. Carol, what are you looking at?" I told her I was trying to see my house. We had become quite good friends since she took care of Mamie Owensby before she died. "When you go back to America," Yvette said, "you must listen to the radio and the TV so you'll know what happens, so you won't forget us."

The pilot of our LIAT plane flew along the coast so everyone aboard could get one last look at the volcano. And then began the flight across the water to Antigua and the plane that was to take us to Puerto Rico and then on to Miami, Chicago and Indianapolis.

27
THE LAST "BOCK-UP"

As we re-entered our lives in Indiana, the volcano seemed quite far away, but the fate of our island and its people was a nagging worry. And what would happen to Paradise East? There was nothing we could do except wait. We immediately signed up for Internet access so we could learn in real time, or with a slight delay, what was happening on the island. I must admit we were horrified to learn that ash flows reached the sea in Spanish Point in early August.

By September, blocks of hot rock fell on Long Ground, damaging many houses and setting others on fire. Several burned to the ground. The Owensbys' Pentecostal church was gutted. And a pyroclastic flow overran the Tar River Estate House. Only the walls of the house were standing, according to the Internet report.

And so it went all during the winter of 1996 and the early spring of 1997, when our insurance company announced it would reduce our coverage to 55 percent as of June. Ed, who was in the insurance business for many years, said this was legal, but, he thought, immoral. The worst case scenario, Ed and I agreed, would be for Spanish Point to remain in the evacuated zone, but our house not be destroyed. We couldn't collect on our insurance—the reduced portion we had left— but we couldn't stay in the house either. In any case, we had resigned ourselves to not going back to stay on Montserrat, certainly not in the near future, and maybe never.

During May, volcanic activity shifted to the East-Southeast of the dome, a relief for us, but a recent report said there had been a mud flow in Tree Top River, which sent 20 inches of mud down a ghaut as far as Trant's, the little village near the airport. Scientists had been saying right along that the airport was safe. Like so many pronounce-ments, that one wasn't true either.

A few days later, a pyroclastic flow boiled down Tuitt's ghaut all the way to the New Redeem Bakery in Tuitt's, where the old man used to wait for his food from Meals on Wheels. And we waited to see what would happen next.

There was a bombshell announcement on June 19: A friend from Montserrat e-mailed us that representatives from the three insurance companies with coverages on the island had met during the week and decided that as of August 1 property insurance on houses south of the Belham River, including us in Spanish Point and in areas in the West such as Iles Bay, Fox's Bay, Cork Hill, Plymouth and St. Georges Hill, would be cancelled completely. This meant that more than half the property of the population of Montserrat would not be covered by insurance after August 1.

The worst was that the companies were removing not only vol-cano coverage but also hurricane. Ed wrote a letter to our company saying we had paid thousands of dollars in premiums and now when we needed the insurance, they were backing out. Since the compa-nies put out a joint statement, many people were particularly miffed because of what seemed like collusion. In a moment of black humor, Ed and I agreed that, if we prayed for anything, we should pray that if the house were going to be destroyed, as we were almost sure it would be, it should happen before August 1.

On June 25, 1997, a huge pyroclastic flow entered Mosqui-to Ghaut near our house, blasting through Bethel, destroying the Methodist church and then down into Spanish Point. A new fam-ily, who had bought a concrete-block house across from the church and intended to farm on the island, remained in their house despite repeated warnings. As the pyroclastic flow rolled down the ghaut at 100 miles an hour they ran to the side of their house the farthest from the volcano. The parents were unscathed, but their daughter, age 5, was slightly burned in the inferno.

We learned via the Internet that a surge of hot gases had obliter-ated Trant's; nothing was left standing. The Anglican church, where bats had flown overhead while our choir was singing in a concert, was destroyed as were many houses in Harris'. We thought all this surely meant that our house was no more, but did not yet know for sure. The next day, at least four deaths were reported, three in a house in Farms Village. The Internet report said about 25 people were still missing. There were numerous rescues by helicopter; one flew in from Guadeloupe and another from a Dutch ship at sea nearby.

Lucy's house was gone as was the Lindls'. Bramble and Bethel villages, where Margaret, Sharon, Angie and Medford lived, totally destroyed. The Methodist manse, whose roof Ed helped repair after Hurricane Hugo, destroyed. It was reported that ash was 15 feet deep in places. Still no definitive word on our house.

The woman who sold vegetables outside Ram's Supermarket refused to leave her house in Harris' and burned to death. The same dreadful end was suffered by a man who worked at the airport. When he left his home in Trant's that morning, he forgot his wallet, but went home to retrieve it, just as pyroclastic flows reached the village.

Without photos of our house or other proof that it had been destroyed, we couldn't file an insurance claim. So we hired Wilma to go into the area as soon as it was allowed to take pictures. So far, the ash had been too hot. By early July, Wilma had arranged with a helicopter pilot to fly over the area so she could take still photos of destroyed homes for seven Spanish Pointers who hired her for the purpose. She also was able to obtain claim forms for the three insurance companies that wrote policies on the island. The companies had announced earlier that, in the event of a loss, they would pay off with a photograph as proof, as long as the loss occurred before August 1.

Over the 4th of July, we were in Michigan staying with some good friends who had visited us on the island and watched a National Geographic special on the recent violent events at Montserrat's volcano. At one point, film taken from a helicopter was shown of our neighborhood. There was a dramatic few seconds of a structure with its back end engulfed in flames. "That's your house!" one of our friends said. We had to agree. Even though the image flashed by rapidly, we could clearly see the bend in the road where our house was located and the swimming pool just inside the fence. If there had ever been any doubt or wishful thinking, there no longer was. Our odyssey at Paradise East was over.

Ed called a friend in Indianapolis, who agreed to videotape the National Geographic special when it was aired there one hour later. Several days afterward, using his VCR's freeze frame capability, we confirmed our suspicions. Wilma's photographs arrived in the mail soon after. The flows had come straight down the ghauts, including the one to the immediate south of our property. The hot gases in that one had obviously set our roof on fire. Another photo showed that

the inside of the house was gutted, including, no doubt, all the furniture I had reupholstered and the newly painted vanity and chest of
drawers. The four walls, made of concrete block, were still standing.

EPILOGUE

In September of 1997 the volcano erupted again, completely burying the Bethel Methodist Church with its tall steeple. Also gone were the remains of our house and the houses of almost everyone who called Spanish Point home. We were told later that, in some places, the ash was forty feet deep.

When we returned to the island the following year to look at the devastation, we stood on Jack Boy Hill looking down at Spanish Point. There were no landmarks at all, except three houses down by the ocean that miraculously escaped the inferno. Otherwise, there were no trees, no roads, no houses, just a gray ash slope dotted with boulders the size of cars.

Some of the people who lived in the East with us left the island for good. Some went to Canada, some to England, some to the United States and some to other Caribbean islands. Some people stayed on Montserrat, re-establishing their lives in the West and North where tropical vegetation remained lush as if nothing had happened. In time, a new capital was built in scattered areas of the North, and a new Montserrat airport opened to replace the one destroyed by the volcano.

Eruptions come and go, continuing to plague the island since that first vent in the East opened up and belched hot water and boulders in July of 1995. No one knows when the activity will end.

As for us, we have gone on with our lives, but we still remember the winters on Montserrat as some of our happiest times.

MORE MONTSERRAT RECIPES

Iguana

Skin and clean a fat female iguana, preferably in March or April, saving the eggs (including the yellow ones), liver and heart. Split the body along the back bone and divide each half in three; divide the legs in two. Boil the eggs in very salty water, seasoned with a chili pepper, for 1/2 hour. Drain.

Meanwhile, sauté the pieces gently in oil until lightly browned. Cover with boiling water, adding a hot pepper, garlic, salt and pepper to taste. Add the eggs, including the shells, and the diced heart and liver. Simmer until most of the liquid has cooked away. Serve by pouring remaining broth over a bed of rice and red beans, heaping the meat on top. From the *Montserrat Cookbook*, published in 1973 to benefit the Old People's Welfare Association.

Duckana (called Conkies in Barbados)

1/2 cup flour
3/4 pound raw pumpkin, grated
4 ounces butter
2 ounces shortening
1/2 pound raw sweet potato, grated
1 cup grated coconut
1 teaspoon salt
3/4 pound brown sugar
2 cups milk
1 teaspoon allspice
1/2 teaspoon nutmeg
almond extract - a splash
raisins, optional
Banana leaves or aluminum foil about 8 inches square

Mix coconut, pumpkin, sweet potato, sugar, spices, almond extract, flour and salt. Stir in melted butter, shortening and milk and mix until smooth. (The Barbados recipe calls for a cup of cornmeal along with the flour. The Montserrat recipe doesn't.) Spoon two heaping tablespoons of the Duckana mixture onto the banana leaf or foil. If on the leaf, roll up and tie with string. Or, wrap in foil. Steam on a rack over boiling water until firm and cooked. This might take an hour.

(This recipe is from various sources)

ABOUT THE AUTHOR...

Carol Elrod was a reporter and feature writer for *The Indianapolis Star* for 14 years. But she had been a writer years before that: she met her husband, Ed, while they were both working on the newspaper and yearbook at Broad Ripple High School in Indianapolis. She studied journalism at Indiana University and earned a master's degree from Ball State University. After their marriage, the Elrods lived in Germany while Ed served in the United States Army. During the 1960s, they and their two children built a cabin in the woods of Brown County in Indiana and in the 1970s rehabilitated a derelict house in downtown Indianapolis. The Montserrat island experience was a highlight of their lives. The couple now lives on Pine Island, Florida.

(Editor's note: The editor and publisher of this book was also a member of the yearbook/newspaper staff at Broad Ripple High at the time Carol and Ed were helping win national awards for the high school publications. It has been said that "Everything we ever need to know about writing we can learn on a good high school newspaper." Nancy Niblack Baxter)